FOR GIVE NESS

for Everyone

FOR GIVE NESS
for Everyone

A Path to Letting Go and Moving Forward

DOUGLAS WEISS, Ph.D

Forgiveness for Everyone: A Path to Letting Go and Moving Forward
Copyright © 2025 by Douglas Weiss

Requests for information:
Discovery Press
heart2heart@xc.org
(719) 278-3708

All rights reserved. No part of this publication may be reproduced, stored in a retrieval system, or transmitted in any form by any means, electronic, mechanical, photocopy, recording, or otherwise, without the prior permission of the publisher, except as provided by USA copyright law.

No patent liability is assumed with respect to the use of the information contained herein. Although every precaution has been taken in the preparation of this book, the publisher and author assume no responsibility for errors or omissions. Neither is any liability assumed for damages resulting from the use of the information contained herein.

Published by Forefront Books, Nashville, Tennessee.
Distributed by Simon & Schuster.

Unless otherwise indicated, Scripture quotations are from the Holy Bible, New International Version®, NIV®, Copyright © 1973, 1978, 1984, 2011 by Biblica, Inc.™ Used by permission of Zondervan. All rights reserved worldwide.

Scripture quotations marked ESV are from the ESV® Bible (The Holy Bible, English Standard Version®), copyright ©2001 by Crossway, a publishing ministry of Good News Publishers. Used by permission. All rights reserved.

Scripture quotations marked JUB are taken from The Jubilee Bible 2000 (JUB) by Ransom Press International. Used by permission. All rights reserved.

Scripture quotations marked KJV are from the King James Version. Public domain.

Scripture quotations marked NKJV are from the New King James Version®. ©1982 by Thomas Nelson. Used by permission. All rights reserved.

Library of Congress Control Number: 2024927017

Print ISBN: 9781637634394
E-book ISBN: 9781637634400

Cover Design by Bruce Gore, Gore Studio, Inc.
Interior Design by PerfecType, Nashville, TN

Printed in the United States of America

CONTENTS

Introduction — 7

Chapter One: The Journey to Peace and Freedom — 9
Chapter Two: Solving the Riddle — 17
Chapter Three: What Am I Forgiving? — 29
Chapter Four: Secret Power — 47
Chapter Five: Me — 69
Chapter Six: First Things First — 97
Chapter Seven: Commanded — 117
Chapter Eight: Everybody Has a Story — 139
Chapter Nine: Boundaries — 161
Chapter Ten: The Trail Less Traveled — 179
Chapter Eleven: Your Tool Box — 199

Christian Resources — 207
About the Author — 227
Notes — 229

INTRODUCTION

Welcome to a brand-new life, seriously! For the last forty years of my life, Monday through Friday, I have been helping individuals and couples work through some of the toughest issues souls can endure. These souls and hearts have been abused, neglected, or abandoned by their parents. They have been sexually abused or raped. The one they married who promised before their families to "forsake all others and to love, honor, and cherish them" cheated on them, spent decades soaking in pornography, or haven't had a physical relationship with them for years or even decades.

These hearts and souls came in Monday to do a five-day intensive counseling, and by Friday, they were able to process the traumas and forgive or be given the tools to forgive. I have countless faces in my mind as I write this seeing them living the Forgiveness for Everyone lifestyle.

I have lived in Colorado Springs for over two decades, and I have found that life is like so many of the trails I have hiked. You have to work to get there, but the views are spectacular. However, you can slip into a ditch and have one of your feet stuck in between a rock and you can't move. You have to find a way out to continue the hike. You can see the peak, but now you feel trapped and unable to reach it.

Forgiveness for Everyone allows you to lift that rock, be no longer trapped, and live the freest life you could ever imagine. Welcome to the adventure!

CHAPTER ONE

The Journey to Peace and Freedom

We are about to embark on one of the most powerfully freeing journeys of your life. Are you ready? Hold on. You are going to feel things you may have never felt before and realize a strength you never knew you had. It's a strength that rises up from inside you, empowering you to do things you previously thought impossible.

It sounds like watching a Hollywood blockbuster. You're sitting on the edge of your seat in the theatre, seeing cinematic characters develop into heroes as the story unfolds. In the beginning of the story, the hero is weak, lost, and uninformed in their great powers. Then, a crisis hits seemingly bigger than they can handle, and they flee to meet some well-informed person and learn about their genealogy or special gift. After going through some highly secret training, "Voilà!" they become heroes saving lives, the world, and maybe even the universe. This is called a *hero epic* and is by far the favorite of moviegoers worldwide.

Our journey, however, is not about a character created out of some writer's imagination in a world that doesn't actually exist. It's a real journey taken by real humans and is one of the most significant journeys that each of us must take, whether we wish to or not. I'm not talking about everyone else either. I am talking about *you*. In this journey we are about to take, you will go face-to-face with your own past and what has specifically happened to you, affecting your heart, your soul, and possibly even your body. You will face the memories of real people in your life who have caused you real pain. But make no mistake about it; you are the hero who is going to climb mountains and travel the valleys or deserts to arrive at the place every soul desires deeply, that place called Peace and Freedom that comes from forgiveness.

This is a lasting peace, not the kind you get from experiencing one of the wonders of the world, sitting by a tranquil lake, strolling a beach at sunset and feeling the ocean's warm breeze, or taking in the fresh fragrance of the forest after a rain. I'm talking about a peace you will be able to have every step of your life, knowing you are free. I mean, *really* free from past hurts or things that have happened to you. At the end of this journey, you will have faced your story; forgiven those in your story, as well as forgiven yourself; and emerged possessing the peace of a clear conscience before God and men. You're not only *experiencing* peace; you are *at* peace. There is a place called Peace and Freedom, but it takes a journey to get there.

A passage in Psalms best describes this journey as God's children. *"Blessed are those whose strength is in you, whose hearts are set on pilgrimage [journey]. As they pass through the Valley of Baka [valley of weeping], they make it a place of springs; the autumn rains also cover it with pools. They go from strength to strength . . ."* (Psalms 84:5–7, emphasis added). When our hearts are set on pilgrimage, when we go through the Valley of Baca, those places of woundedness, God promises to turn them into areas of springs and refreshment, of peace and freedom. The key to walking this passage out in real life is the word *set*. The traveler's heart is set, or fixed, on taking the pilgrimage/journey until the end.

This is the journey every soul will be challenged to take. I have counseled many who have gone all the way through to their journey's end. Some souls, however, fear the journey so much that they cower in the shadows of who they really could become. Some get sidetracked by judgment, bitterness, or the pure distractions of this life, pulling them away from the journey within. After counseling thousands of souls, I've come to solidly believe in our indestructibility as we take this journey. You may feel frail, fragile, or even doubtful, yet by utilizing the tools in the following pages, you can not only confidently arrive at that place of peace and freedom, but you might also receive the calling to help others along this journey of forgiveness that is for everyone.

For a couple of decades, I've been blessed to live in Colorado Springs. What I've discovered over the years is the people who live here are some of the most adventurous, outdoor-loving people in the country. They climb mountains for entertainment on the weekends, often scaling thousands of feet before breakfast. They go whitewater rafting in frigid water, camp out in the snow, and rappel off the sides of rocky cliffs. You get it. Here is my point: Usually, on these types of adventures, you are introduced to a particular person before you start. The group gathers around this person called your *guide*.

Now, a guide is a unique kind of person. He or she loves what they do so much, they do it thousands of times and help thousands of people go from point A to point B. The really good guides have a knack for getting you excited as you climb, camp, or raft. They paint the adventure so beautifully, telling the glories of the journey about to be taken to those they are leading, that even a sane person would want to take the journey. Their joy for their particular expedition is so contagious, you almost want to give up your responsible life and go be a guide for a few years. Then, of course, they warn you of the possibly dangerous aspects that you could face, like injuries or death, and how to best prevent these from happening to you. Finally, there is the last part of the guide's discussion, which is critical to the entire experience. The guide will tell you a little bit about their own story, which makes them flawed, lovable, courageous, and slightly more trustworthy as they are transparent and vulnerable with themselves and with you.

On this journey you are taking through these pages, I will be your guide. My prayer is that I will be a good one. As your guide, it's my responsibility to share my own story to reassure you that I have traveled the road of forgiveness for decades. Also, I have helped countless people travel the various terrains of forgiveness and am more than qualified to take you through your own journey of Forgiveness for Everyone.

My Story

My story starts before I was born. My mother had an affair during her first marriage, and I was conceived as a result of that adultery. This led to her first divorce, while being pregnant. Being a single mother back in the early 1960s with only an eighth-grade education and virtually no job skills meant living in poverty. She met a man in a bar, and he married her, pregnant and all. His last name was Weiss. They stayed married for a handful of years and had three more daughters before his alcoholism killed that marriage. Being single with three other children, she couldn't provide. Destitute and without support from her own family, she put us four children in foster homes. I remember going to several of these homes as a little guy. Eventually, my mother was able to convince the social worker she and her new live-in boyfriend could provide for us. Together, they got each of us out of our separate foster care homes.

We had no books in our house during my junior high years. My mother, however, somehow purchased a human sexuality college textbook and gave it to me to read. I don't remember reading much, but the pictures started what would become a sexual addiction for years. Around that same time, I was walking across town one early evening, and a man offered me a ride, gave me alcohol, got me very drunk, and sexually abused me. This led to much promiscuity with women for years. The alcohol and drugs were becoming a habit to cover the neglect in the home, the sexual abuse, and the lack of any spiritual life.

At nineteen, I realized my life was going nowhere, and I knew if I kept going the way I was, I would only leave a trail of self-destruction and suffering for those around me. Years prior, at twelve, I'd been sent off to a Salvation Army camp, where I'd gone down the aisle to accept Christ as my Savior. After that the Holy Spirit never let me go, and at nineteen, I still knew Jesus was God. Late one night at another church campground with nobody else around, I knelt down and said, "Jesus, I know you are God. I will give you my life 100 percent and do whatever you say for thirty days, and if my life is not improved by then, I will kill myself." I was just being raw and real with God. He heard my prayer, and shortly thereafter, I enrolled in Bible school.

At Bible school, the pastor of a large church attempted to sexually abuse me. He was later found guilty of sexually abusing several young men and destroyed the church I had grown to love. After seminary and starting my career, a deacon of my church got me involved in a Ponzi scheme, and I lost all of my savings. He served years in jail for all the people he swindled.

Professionally, I have had several professional counselors from well-known ministries attack me and my work. People have viciously lied about me. I have gone through several betrayals of people I loved, trained, and economically blessed significantly. They were all professing Christians. Half of my pastors over the years have fallen to sexual sin. There are other stories of people with whom I have had to make the journey of forgiving so I could be at peace and free from their sin in my life.

The trail God has led me on has resulted in a number of insights that have helped me and many of my clients as well. The tools that I will share with you in the following chapters are tried and true. I personally and professionally know they will work when actually applied to your own journey as you go through these pages with me as your guide.

CHAPTER TWO

Solving the Riddle

Let's start our journey together with a little riddle. Ready? Here goes:

What is present on any journey of a thousand miles, yet is also present just going to the store, church, or gym? You come across it frequently and have to go through it to arrive at your destination.

Do you know the answer? Here are some hints.

1. It's shaped like an octagon.
2. It has to be obeyed.
3. It is red.
4. It says STOP on it.

You got it: a stop sign! Okay, I know that was a no-brainer, way too easy. I did it because, on this journey, we have to start with the stop signs. But why there? That seems like an odd place to begin a journey of forgiveness. I mean, to get to our destination, we need green lights, not stop signs. Why not start with some big theological point about forgiveness and how we must do it, or something like it? We'll certainly get to some of those things later, but for now, as a psychologist, if I can help you acknowledge a few of the stop signs in your life, you might be able to arrive at your destination much quicker, safer, and without a collision somewhere on your journey early on. Stop signs are meant for you to stop, look both ways, and keep on driving to get wherever you are going. Some people, though, after they hit one of these stop signs on the road to forgiveness, instead of driving through, stay stopped because they give in to denial, anger, judgment, depression, pessimism, bitterness, and the fear of trusting others again. Instead of living life to the fullest, they hide in the shadows of what was done in the past, staying wounded rather than getting healed. They become stuck or run out of gas in that place.

That does not have to describe you or me. Today is a new day! In this second chapter, we are going to acknowledge these stop signs and, I hope, allow you to get an easier start to your journey called Forgiveness for Everyone.

These stop signs that we must encounter are beliefs we have in our hearts. No doubt, defying stop signs can be fatal, but not moving on past them can be as well. We encounter them to deal with them. The one thing I have learned for certain after counseling souls for almost four decades is that if someone believes something with all their heart, they will behave in accordance with their beliefs, even if they are false assumptions.

For example, if someone believes they are worthless, they will believe and make choices based upon being worthless. But when the light of truth is revealed and received, they will be free. *"And you shall know the truth, and the truth shall make you free"* (John 8:32 NKJV). The truth is, they are worth the blood of Christ because He says so—and the same is true for you. *"But God demonstrates His own love toward us, in that while we were still sinners, Christ died for us"* (Romans 5:8 NKJV). The Creator of life loves you so intensely that He allowed His own Son to die in your place before you ever repented. Forgiveness for us resided in the heart of God from the beginning.

If you believe one of these following stop signs, you will behave as you believe and will be stuck—limited on your journey of forgiveness simply because you believe something that is not true at all. So, if you hit a stop sign that you have held on to, please consider letting it go and embracing the truth that will set you free.

Stop Sign #1: I Have to Confront Them in Order to Forgive Them

When someone holds this belief, they may cling to unforgiveness for years or an entire lifetime. The belief is that the perpetrator of the abuse, neglect, heartbreak, slander, or flat-out lying, the one who damaged you emotionally, physically, spiritually, sexually, or even financially, is someone you must go toe to toe with in order to forgive them.

Although someone might deeply and truly believe this, there are no scriptural demands for it. I know the scripture tells us that if another believer sins against you, go privately and [deal with] the offense (Matthew 8:15). However, there is no command that we must confront someone in order to forgive that person for anything they have done to us.

Here is the problem with believing this stop sign on your journey to forgiveness. First, if this has happened in your past, you may never be able to locate the person(s) to confront them. According to this stop sign, that would mean you couldn't forgive them. Second, they could be dead, as many of my clients have had a parent, sexual perpetrator, or bully die way before it was possible to confront them, or the client was not old enough or emotionally strong enough to forgive them.

Third, as I alluded to, especially with severe trauma, even thinking of them and what happened could trigger strong feelings of fear, hopelessness, or powerlessness, and you could shut down in their presence or, worse, be victimized by their response to you or by their blaming you for their perpetration in your life. This has happened to multiple clients of mine who confronted their perpetrator prior to seeing me. Many were re-traumatized by the response, denial, or attempts to blame them (the victim) for what their perpetrator had done.

I'll never forget Suzie, a bright, successful businesswoman in her thirties with two daughters. She had been sexually abused by her uncle on and off for years and believed her parents knew about it and did nothing. She was deeply traumatized by the sexual trauma, as well as by her parents' lack of intervention. Suzie was at the funeral of a family member, and she thought this uncle might be there. She believed that she would finally confront him about the years of sexual abuse. Suzie pulled him aside after the funeral and did exactly what she had done numerous times in her imagination. Two things happened that she didn't expect: her feelings, and his response. She didn't expect to feel so small and weak in his presence, making it hard to communicate what she wanted to say. She did manage to tell him that what he had done to her all those years was wrong. However, she wasn't ready for his sociopathic response. "You wanted to do that, and you actually asked me to do that to you. You were a wild little girl that liked doing that with me." When she heard those words, Suzie shut down immediately. She had to leave the funeral and then went into a deep depression before she came to me for counseling. Over time we were able to get her to assign full responsibility to the perpetrator and begin to heal from the trauma. She forgave him without re-confronting him, and today she is living a thriving life.

If you are determined to confront someone about a particular behavior, here's my advice. First, go through all these pages ahead of you so you are stronger before you do that. Second, speak to a counselor to prepare and role-play for the worst possible response so you are not expecting the other person to automatically agree with you. Even though you are telling the truth, they may still be in denial or defensive about what occurred.

Stop Sign #2: They Have to Ask Me for Forgiveness in Order for Me to Forgive

"Well, when my mom comes to me and asks to be forgiven for physically beating me, shaming me, and making me the scapegoat for her awful life, sure, doc, I'll forgive, but not until then."

Charlie, a forty-eight-year-old deacon, spilled his woundedness to me as we were starting down his journey of forgiving everyone. Having every right to feel abused, he'd been beaten constantly by his alcoholic single mother, who never got over her husband's affair and subsequent divorce. He was humiliated constantly, not only by their poverty, but by her showing up drunk, or not showing up, and his having to walk miles home. Charlie was in severe pain, and he believed with all his heart his mom had to repent before he could forgive her.

I have worked with thousands of women whose husbands were addicted to porn or had multiple affairs, and each one wanted their recently caught, physically fifty-year-old but emotionally fourteen-year-old husband, to sincerely repent and realize the pain he had put her through. However, because of his addiction and emotional immaturity, he simply wasn't capable of it at that moment. He could say he was sorry, but that deep-felt repentance would come about eight to twelve months into recovery, when he could actually feel with empathy the pain he had caused. Was she to simply wait until he grew up? What if he never grew up? She could be stuck at this stop sign for quite a while, even if he was recovering from his addiction.

There are a couple of problems when you truly believe this stop sign—that they have to ask you for forgiveness before you can forgive them. First, only a small percentage of people are actually mature enough to see their own sin, go to the one they have wounded, and take full responsibility for their sin perpetrated against the other person. Take a moment and consider the thousands of sins you've committed versus the times you went and asked for forgiveness. It humbles us when we think about the significant difference between those two realities.

I'll never forget being a young believer in Christ, maybe a year old in the Lord, when I went to a Christian conference. The speaker suggested we make a list of people we had hurt or harmed and go face-to-face with them, repent, and actually ask them to forgive us. There were about five thousand believers in attendance, so I assumed he knew what he was talking about. Shortly afterward, I made my list of people whom I felt I had harmed and went face-to-face with as many as I could locate. I'll always remember several of the responses during this process of asking people to forgive me, such as, "I have never had anyone ask me to forgive them before." Now, I think not too many people actually go around asking forgiveness for those people they hurt. To expect your list of people to come and ask you for forgiveness could keep you at this stop sign for years, possibly the rest of your life, and that would truly be sad.

Second, the problem with this belief is that you give all the power to the perpetrator as to whether you will experience the freedom that forgiveness brings you. Why would any rational person give anyone who was unwise or just plain wicked or uncaring enough to do such a thing to you any power over your life or freedom? The people who hurt you were perhaps immature, and we've all been there in our lives. They could be unsympathetic or just lack insight into themselves. We all know that person who can never be wrong or say they are sorry. Your perpetrator may also be wicked, evil, or have any number of psychological disorders prohibiting them from having much insight or self-awareness. So again, why would you give them the power to drive your car and suffer any of the consequences in your life from unforgiveness?

You will discover beyond any doubt that you are absolutely able to forgive without them being present or ever asking you for forgiveness. This truth gives you the ability to forgive anyone of anything without their cooperation at all. Right now, I can vividly picture so many faces of my clients after they realized they could forgive without the other person's involvement. How much brighter and lighter they looked when they actually did the things that are written on the following pages. It makes me excited for your journey of forgiveness.

Stop Sign #3: They Have to Change Before I Forgive Them

I agree that in a perfect world, especially for those of us who follow Christ, it would be so awesome if, when someone sinned against us, they would come and take responsibility, ask for forgiveness, and then never commit that behavior again. If you have lived on this incredible planet for very long, you might have realized that this is not always the case, for sure. I'll be the first to agree it would be good for them and all the people they love if they would stop their hurtful behavior permanently. As a Christian psychologist who's counseled people for almost four decades, I have come to believe, even of myself, that change is first a commitment and then a process to arrive at. For me, it would take intentionality, focus, and often accountability to see a change in behavior I didn't like inside of me. If you look at yourself—whether your struggle is anger, being on time, patience, or something else—you see that it takes time to change. Should someone not forgive you as you mature in that area?

People change either when the Holy Spirit convicts them deeply, when they experience severe consequences, or from peer pressure. Making change a prerequisite for you to forgive, like with stop sign number two, allows the other person to drive your car instead of you driving your car. The truth is, you have the power to forgive whether they ever change or not. You might need to set boundaries if they don't change or even end the relationship. However, you don't have to give them your power to forgive them. That is 100 percent yours, and you can use it any time you want for anyone you want. It's your gift, and nobody has to change one iota for you to fully forgive and walk free from any sins they have committed against you.

Going Through the Stop Signs

When you are going to your favorite destination, be it the beach, the mountains, work, or the gym, you will encounter several stop signs along the way. These signs are there to keep you safe and to help those on the roads move along in an orderly manner. You might have encountered one, two, or all three of the above stop signs while traveling on your journey of trying to forgive those in your past who may have caused you pain. However, if you have been stopped for a while at any of these stop signs on your road to forgiveness, it's time to grip the wheel and drive through them, fully embracing the road ahead of you. It could feel somewhat uncomfortable or even frightening to forgive, just like I have felt looking at a mountain we are about to climb. Yet, by taking one step at a time as the guide leads us, we'll see many splendid things and have a great sense of accomplishment when we reach the summit. It's an incredibly breathtaking view you only get by being on top of a mountain.

That is my wish for you as you follow along a tried-and-true path that so many have already taken with life-altering results. There's a freedom their heart had never experienced before and results they couldn't even explain. This is not only possible for you but probable if you stay on the path and do the work that's ahead of you to forgive everyone.

CHAPTER THREE

What Am I Forgiving?

"Dr. Weiss, I have been a believer for a long time, over thirty years," Rodney says to me. He's come for a five-day counseling intensive. "I know that I'm supposed to forgive," he continues. "I have had a whole lot of stuff happen to me; some I think I brought on myself, so what exactly am I supposed to be forgiving here?"

Rodney was right; he had endured a lot of physical abuse from his dad and older brother. He was never protected by his mother, who was cold and disconnected from him. He was bullied at school and then hit by a drunk driver at twenty, which took a year to recover from. His first and second wife cheated on him—in one case, with one with his best friends—just to mention a little of what he had gone through in his life.

Rodney was intelligent and owned a successful business with several employees. His porn addiction was what brought him to me, but boy, he was going to need to travel the road to forgiveness. Jacked up emotionally, he could not share a feeling. He was angry and had no real life other than his work. Rodney was one of many clients I would see who, to some degree, didn't even realize what he was supposed to forgive people for. Not because he wasn't bright, but because he didn't have a language for what he was actually forgiving because Rodney's abuse, neglect, and betrayal were his everyday life.

You might be in the same boat. I know I was. I didn't really know what neglect was until after I was counseling others for a while. I didn't realize that much of what I had experienced after getting saved were things I really needed to take the journey of forgiveness on, but I did, and I am glad I did.

So, what are we forgiving? One thing we are forgiving is the SIN that others have done to us, and that simple three-letter word has so many different manifestations. Some of these sins are willful in that the other person didn't care if you got hurt by their behavior, or maybe they were intentionally trying to hurt you with their behavior. Others have sinned against you because they are human sinners, and that's what sinners do.

They sin, and sin hurts people. They could be completely unaware of how their actions affected you and had no intention to cause pain, but nonetheless, it was a sin, and you got hurt.

This journey of forgiving everyone is precarious, to say the least. Most believers know that we are all sinners and realize our personal need for forgiveness for big and little stuff. Yet we are also called upon by our Creator to forgive sin in its various manifestations. Let's look at these various manifestations through a few different lenses.

Scripture says that sin came through Adam and infected the entire human race (Romans 5:12–19). However, since the Law, we now had a way to know we were sinning against God and others (Romans 3:19). Just a quick breeze through the Ten Commandments would give us something to think about. The first command is not to have other gods. You know, material things, like social media, entertainment, and work—modern-day idols. We are not to take His name in vain but keep His name sacred. Keep the Sabbath, honor your parents, don't kill, don't cheat on your spouse, don't steal, don't bear false witness, and don't lust after your neighbor's spouse or their material things. This is the big stuff, and you may have had some of these happen against you.

Things like betrayal, lying, stealing, and being lied about would be pretty normal stuff on the forgiveness journey, for sure. However, I have been counseling people for quite a while now, and it's absolutely mind-boggling some of the more inhumane things I've seen them go through. I want to share some key thoughts about abuse and neglect that might help you put words to some of your experiences. Words you might have to consider on your journey to Forgiveness for Everyone.

Types of Experiences

These experiences of abuse and neglect vary in intensity and frequency. For some, it was a family member, and for others, it was a complete stranger. The duration of such events can range from a one-time experience all the way to many years, even decades. You and your story are unique, and the way you have stuffed, denied, medicated, or processed these experiences is also unique. Why am I saying this? It's because you can't compare your wounds or reactions to anyone else's wounds or reactions. There is no room for any "shoulding" on yourself in the journey of forgiving everyone, or on when or how you "should" process your pains.

We are going to travel quickly through this vast terrain of human experiences, and not all will apply to you, but enough will be applicable to help you have clarity as you do the work ahead of you. During this leg of the journey, I will frequently zigzag between abuse and neglect. In my experience, those are different sides of the same coin. Our research has also borne this out. For example, in my book *Partner Betrayal Trauma*, we did a study of women.[1] What we found out in a nutshell is that, statistically, the women who had experienced porn/sex addiction or infidelity from their husbands had the same experience as the women who experienced intimacy anorexia from their husbands, which is the active withholding of spiritual, emotional, and/or sexual intimacy. These women from both sides of the same coin had remarkably similar scores on depression as well as other symptoms of post-traumatic stress disorder. So, as I mention a topic of abuse, I will also discuss the neglect side because so often, the neglect can be as damaging (if not more so) to the soul than the active abuse.

Physical Abuse and Neglect

When we are talking about physical abuse, we are talking about what has happened with or toward your body from others. The physical abuse is relatively easy to explain. Here, you were hit, pushed, held against your will, beaten, and more. You might have been forced to do things way beyond your capabilities. You may have been punished in a cruel and unusual manner. I worked with a client who was placed in a dog cage as a form of punishment.

I'll never forget Steve, who, when we started the journey of forgiveness, said, "Doc, I am willing to forgive and know I have to forgive my dad, but what am I supposed to do with these?" As he spoke, he rolled up his sleeve and showed me the scars from his dad punishing him by pressing lit cigarettes into his forearms. If you have been physically abused, you will want to take the journey to forgive those who have done these things to you.

Now, let's zag into physical neglect. This would be you not being fed regularly, not being touched affectionately on a regular basis, no hugs or holding your hands, not being cared for in an appropriate manner when you were sick, and having dental or medical needs that went unaddressed. Physical neglect can happen at any socioeconomic level. It is real and can impact your value of yourself in a significant manner for years or decades.

Emotional Abuse and Neglect

Emotional abuse can be yelling at you, being constantly critical of you, calling you negative names, and shaming you for things you have done or things you can't change, such as looking like the other parent.

Emotional neglect is the silence that was so loud in your house. It was withholding praise from you after a major accomplishment or when you worked hard and got all A's but one B on your report card. The refusal to praise you to family members or others is also neglect. Silence can be abusive. The lack of affirmation of you and your uniqueness can have a lifelong impact on you.

I'll never forget Candace, who grew up in such a home of emotional neglect. "Dr. Weiss, I would give anything to hear my dad say, 'I love you' or 'I'm proud of you,' and now he is dead." She was a globally known businesswoman who had never heard "I love you" from her father, and that was neglectful. Once in Bible college, I was on a pay phone (those of you who are old enough can remember putting coins in them) making a call to my stepdad. I was probably twenty-one or twenty-two, and as I was about to hang up, he said, "I love you." I remember getting off the phone, and it occurred to me that I had never heard those words from any man before in my life. That's emotional neglect, and yes, I forgave them decades ago.

Spiritual Abuse and Neglect

Spiritual abuse is a challenge to explain. Put simply, I find it is that you were not allowed to have a voice in your spiritual life. If it was religious abuse, you may have been asked or demanded to believe or behave in a certain way. Each religion or cult has different ways this could happen. As one client explained it to me, "The rules were way more important than I ever was." They felt they had to act a certain way to be loved, and if not, love was withheld from one or both parents.

Spiritual neglect is the exact opposite. God in any form was never discussed. Religion was not allowed to be a topic in the family and may have been looked down on as weak. The parents never took a spiritual journey or had been hurt by religion, so you grew up in a spiritual vacuum with no thoughts about God in any particular matter.

Sexual Abuse and Neglect

Sexual abuse has been a much-talked-about subject in the last several decades. Sexual abuse is any type of sexual touch, behavior, or penetration of a minor, or of an adult without consent, which is often called rape. Your sexuality is a sacred part of yourself that is unique to you but is integral to who you are. I have heard every form of sexual abuse you can imagine. Often, the victim of sexual abuse will blame themselves before assigning full responsibility to the perpetrator. Sexual abuse or rape of any kind is trauma, and the responsibility is solely the perpetrator's.

I remember an incident with Britney, whose dad made regular comments about her breasts. She felt humiliated and sexualized by this. Boys who had sex acts with older women can stay in denial for decades, believing they got lucky somehow, but actually, what they experienced was sexual abuse. I'll never forget the story of a client I met in a psychiatric ward, who we will call Bruce. He was there because he was suicidal, and I was assigned to conduct a sexual assessment on him. I asked him why he was in the hospital, and he said he was having affairs with nine women and couldn't take it. I asked him about his first sexual encounter. He told me that at about thirteen years of age, he had gone over to his friend's house to play. His friend wasn't there, but the mom invited him in and had sex with him. This went on several times a week until Bruce was married at thirty-three. All of the women he had affairs with were also twenty or more years older than him. Sexual abuse can have a wide variety of unique symptoms.

Sexual neglect is the exact opposite but also can have huge impacts on you. This is when you are not given any sexual education as your body is changing—erections, periods, wet dreams, or any of these. It could be, like my accountability partner was told, "Sex is bad and nasty, and save it for the one you love." This was the message he received growing up in church and is a twisting of the truth. Negative declarations about sex, like "all men want is sex," send harmful messages about a part of you that you will probably express in some way as an adult. I have known women who didn't even know what sex was until after having it. Sexual neglect leaves you ill-prepared to manage your sexuality in life. It also inhibits the God-given expression of your sexuality in a free, healthy, and emotionally secure marriage.

Abuse and Neglect of Gifts

You might be thinking, *What do gifts have to do with a conversation about abuse?* Well, they have a place in this discussion because I have seen clients impacted by both the abuse and neglect of their gifts. Your gifts, be they athletic, academic, artistic, musical, intellectual, or any type, can be used in an abusive manner. I have known people who have had to practice countless hours a week for most of their childhood and adolescence. The gift becomes all-consuming, your life becomes out of balance, and you don't feel normal. You are asked to go to great lengths to be the best or at the top of your game to the point that the rest of your interests and friends are a far second place. If you have experienced gift abuse, you are usually aware of this.

Gift neglect is also a reality for many. This is when your gifts are not explored, supported, or encouraged in any way. Your parents choose not to invest in your abilities or training that would help your gifts grow. Often, if you discover your gifts later in life, you may experience gift neglect. This would be if you were a closet artist, musician, etc., but were not encouraged to express this or pursue accelerated learning in this area. I remember a child my friends knew who was so gifted in drama, but even though the family was wealthy, they did not believe in investing in this child's talents. You could have also been shamed for your gifts because they were so different from your parents'. Or maybe you were neglected because you had a sibling who was gifted at something that you simply had no interest or gifting in.

I hope this conversation on abuse and neglect helps put some language to what you may have experienced in your life. I find having the words to express what you are feeling is very helpful. Personally, I was over thirty when I realized that the much older adult women who were sexual with me were engaging in sexual abuse toward me. As you have language, you can accept your story and forgive those who need it.

The Problem with Sin

It's foundational here, in the early steps of our journey, that we discuss this problem called *sin*. There are at least three major aspects of sin that are important to examine. Imagine that philosophical interlude you could have as you are surrounded by pine trees while climbing the mountain through the forest. You turn to your friend or a complete stranger, and you have some of the most interesting conversations. In this case, picture you and me walking side by side on the trail, and I say, "So, what are your thoughts about sin?" You probably feel like that's random, or like I do many times on a plane or after speaking at a conference when someone asks a question just so they can share their thoughts with you. So, let's have this conversation about sin as we stroll together.

Well, the first issue with sin is that *we were never created for it or its effects*. In Genesis, when God made Adam out of dirt, He breathed His very own breath into him, making Adam the first eternal being born in time and as sinless as God Himself. And then the Lord told Adam he was free. This act of giving man free will was the greatest risk heaven has ever taken. That is why the earth was created—to hold such an experiment. My point, however, is that Adam was not made to sin. He was given the choice to follow and obey only one rule: Do not eat from the tree of the knowledge of good and evil. Yet, Adam was not designed for sin itself. You can verify this by your own experience.

When you or I sin, we feel guilt, shame, and, if we are sensitive enough, a separation from God that we didn't sense when walking more in obedience to His word. The more we know God intimately and the more we know His word and His desire for our lives, the more we feel these strong emotions. Suppose we rebelliously continue in a pattern of sin. The sense of separation gets worse and worse, so we either have to harden our hearts, medicate these feelings, or do what we have done so many times in our walk with God: confess our sin and repent of our sinful behavior to gain that clean conscience we are truly designed for.

I have worked with thousands of clients from every age, race, and socioeconomic status who have felt such dread for the poor choices they have continued to make, regardless of their faith or lack of it. My conclusion from this is that we were not created to sin and sin continually.

The second issue with sin as we continue walking together, breathing in the sunshine and fresh air, is the fact *we were not designed to be sinned against*. When someone, especially a person close to our heart, sins against us, it can create the most incredible pain imaginable. Let me share with you an experience I have had hundreds of times on Mondays when couples begin a five-day counseling intensive for the husband's sex addiction.

For example, prior to arriving, a husband (let's call him Mark) has told his wife (let's call her Jane) a portion of the story—usually the portion he got caught at already. Mark told her about the pornography he has been viewing in the last year. He got caught on his computer. He also told her about a woman he kissed at a bar when he was out of town three years ago. Jane is already in pain from these sins. However, she doesn't totally believe that's all he did. Her intuition is going crazy. She wants to trust and rebuild the marriage, yet something deep down inside says there is more she doesn't know.

At that point, I ask Mark if he would like help to have his wife trust him again so the marriage can recover and thrive. Mark agrees to take a polygraph (lie detector) test. The three of us create the test questions together. He takes his test, and we find out the porn has been going on for over a decade. He has had sex with six women. One was an affair that lasted almost three years, and the most recent one was only a few weeks earlier.

Jane goes into full-blown trauma right there in the chair. I have seen this so many times. It's as if a lightning bolt hit the top of her head, and her body can't handle the voltage. She convulses and screams like a wild beast who was shot, and this can go on for ten to thirty minutes. You see, Jane was not created to be sinned against, and neither are we. This would be an extreme situation to illustrate my point. However, check your human experience when someone lies about you, betrays you, manipulates or uses you, steals your money or virginity, takes credit for your work, or in some other way intentionally hurts you. Their sin hurts your spirit, soul, and body. Sometimes, you get mad, sad, or even, as I had a client express to me. The point is that we were not designed to be sinned against because God designed us to live in a sinless state.

The third issue with sin that is important to process as we continue is slightly more challenging. That is, *we all sin—every one of us*. You can also compare this to your human experience going way back. If you are having challenges finding examples, just ask your parents, siblings, or spouse. We all struggle with this thing called sin. We manifest it differently. Some of us have struggled with the knowledge of evil that has led us to be immoral, lie, steal, blame, and lack insight into our self-destructiveness. We wrestle with the side of the tree Adam and Eve ate from: the knowledge of evil. Others of us twist the knowledge of good. We are judgmental. We put people in boxes and decide if they are lovable based on self-assigned or religiously based protocols, whether they vote our way or believe our favorite doctrine. We are more self-righteous, leaning on our goodness and keeping the law as we see it as opposed to realizing our darkness and His eternal goodness through Christ.

We are all complicit in this thing called sin. So, how do we manage a process that we are part of at some level? The continuum of showing empathy and compassion, even toward the sickest sinners who are so broken in order to do such things to us, is a struggle, and I have experienced this conundrum myself. So often, we judge them as though we were the Most High ourselves. We will walk through some places later in the book that can help us understand many of these issues as we stay on the path toward Forgiveness for Everyone.

There are times it may feel daunting, but thanks be to God, Christ Himself has forged this path for all of us, and we have the Holy Spirit inside of us urging us on like a friend who knows we can do something. He is smiling with joy as we take steps on this journey through the sin issues into a much better place, which was paid for by Christ and maintainable through the Spirit of God in us through Christ Jesus. That place is where there is literally Forgiveness for Everyone.

CHAPTER FOUR

Secret Power

Whether it's Superman, Captain America, Wonder Woman, or Ant-Man, it seems Americans can't get enough of their superheroes. Every year, billions are spent on movies featuring these larger-than-life characters with otherworldly powers. They fly through the air faster than rockets, stop bullets with their bare hands, throw golden lassos around villains, have X-ray vision, and travel through time, all while eating a taco. Their abilities may vary, but their goals are the same. Stop the bad guys, save the world, and, if necessary, the universe. It's hard to find anyone who doesn't love a great superhero movie. They allow us to escape the day-to-day grind with all its limitations of time and natural energy.

Many times, the superhero starts out as a regular Joe or Jane going through the mundaneness of life like the rest of us. They're dealing with relationship issues, and they are insecure, underappreciated, and struggling to pay their bills. Some are portrayed as failures and outcasts of society. Typically, the early scenes in the movie are so average that you may be tempted to leave the theatre because it feels so much like your own life. Then, at some key moment in the story, "IT" happens. They get bitten by a spider, hit by gamma rays, or injected with some special serum, and "Shazam!" they're transformed into people with herculean abilities that enable them to defeat the world's evil while at the same time working through their personal issues.

There are also superheroes who were born with special powers that were hidden until sometime around high school, when their dormant abilities suddenly began to manifest, creating awkward moments. For example, when this seemingly normal teenager takes up for a weaker kid who's being bullied at school. He punches the bully, expecting him to grab his stomach and back off. Instead, the bully is sent flying through the air and crashing through the brick wall, all while the onlooking students' jaws drop open. Our future superhero, shocked at the power unleashed through his hands, bolts into hiding until coming to grips with this new reality. Finally, he emerges from the shadows with a new calling on his life as the world's protector.

Another way heroes gain their abilities is by stumbling upon an object with superpowers, such as a ring, bracelet, or wand. They then must learn to master its use. These motion pictures are what we call hero epics, and they all involve a human who manifests some superpower and becomes the world's hero.

I once penned a novel titled *Erin: The Last Dragon*. Erin was a teenage girl who transformed into a dragon. In either state, she was stronger than ten men and could not be destroyed by man-made weapons. Neither could she be burned, and she had the unusual ability to see inside a person's heart, discerning if it was pure or dark. Erin was in high school trying to figure out male relationships. While writing the manuscript, I had to study the two major movie types: the epic hero and the tragic hero.

Believe it or not, we're going somewhere with all this—somewhere that's going to be "super" helpful in our journey of Forgiveness for Everyone. Before we go any further, though, let's take a moment to sit and warm ourselves around the campfire by the lake we found on our mountainside. While kicking back and listening to the flames crackle, we'll also enjoy a little discussion before moving on to the harder parts of our journey.

Both the epic hero and the tragic hero themes have quite a bit to do with superpowers and the single superpower you were given when you accepted Jesus as your Lord and Savior.

The epic hero theme of literature generally goes as follows: Your character either accidentally discovers that they have a superpower, or it is revealed to them by someone from another dimension. The future hero stumbles a bit with the new revelation but then meets the advanced race, tribe, or Merlin-type mentor, and someone or a group takes them under their wings. The hero goes through some Yoda-and-Luke-Skywalker training. After that, the hero is faced with the seemingly impossible task of saving the world or universe. Of course, doing so always requires the mastering and use of their superpowers. In the end, the world is safe, and its citizens can resume a life of peace. As an added benefit, the hero's relationship struggles are healed, usually sealed with a long and passionate kiss.

The hero tragic theme in literature is strikingly similar to the hero epic theme. In both, the hero is bumbling through life, ignorant of their superpower, or the superpower event has yet to happen. At the critical point in the story, they discover they are the "chosen one" with a superpower and a destiny mission. They fumble around for a while, coming to grips before meeting the tribe, mentor, or other supers who guide and train them.

Here's where the two themes diverge from one another. The hero is trained and given the opportunity to fulfill their mission. Instead of stepping up, however, they cower back and don't use their gifts to accomplish the task. They fail themselves and everyone else. There are all kinds of losses and sufferings because of their failure. Sometimes, the hero even dies running from their destiny. This is a hero tragic movie.

In both narratives, they were special and capable; they fumbled but then were trained. One applied what they learned in their training, and the other didn't, creating opposite results. One saved the world while the other lost it, costing them and so many others. As you take your journey of forgiving everyone, you will be equipped to use your superpowers. I earnestly pray that you will use your training and become the hero in your own story.

No Others

I want to walk you through how God has withheld this secret power throughout time, trusting no one with this tremendous gift until He Himself came to the earth in Christ. Noah, who was found righteous in the sight of God, was entrusted to build the ark and save humanity from destruction, but he was not given this gift. Abraham believed in God and was counted as righteous. He was called the friend of God and given land, great wealth, and influence. Through Abraham's seed, God would birth His family and eventually bring forth the Messiah. Yet, Abraham was not trusted with this superpower.

Joseph was second only to Pharaoh and kept the family of Israel alive during a great famine, but he was not given this superpower. Moses was also called a friend of God and met with Him regularly. Through Moses, the Lord did mighty miracles, and even appeared to him as a burning bush. Moses was given the law, which is the basis of our Western culture, but he was not given this superpower. King David, a man after God's own heart who fought lions and bears, slayed giants, wrote and sang majestic songs, won historic victories, and was the beloved king of Israel, also was not empowered by this gift. His son Solomon, the richest and wisest man who ever lived prior to Christ, was not handed this gift by the Father God. None of the kings of Israel and Judah were given this superpower. Neither were the great prophets like

Isaiah, Ezekiel, Jeremiah, and all the minor prophets given the superpower that God would eventually release into time.

John the Baptist leapt inside his mother's womb when pregnant Mary walked into the room. He preached repentance and baptized thousands, and Jesus Himself said there was none greater born of a woman than John the Baptist. Yet not even John the Baptist was given this gift. Not a single one of the greatest men and women of Scripture, prior to Jesus, was given this superpower from heaven. Not only were they not given this incredible gift, but they couldn't even imagine this gift coming from God that would change world history. This superpower was hidden in God until Jesus Christ walked among us, was able to carry the gift, and then released this superpower to men and women. At this perfect time in history's story, mankind was in the most desperate need of this gift.

Jesus and the Superpower

Jesus revealed this superpower during His earthly ministry. Most of the time, however, when He manifested it, people got upset, particularly the religious crowd. If you've watched many superhero movies, then you know well that there's usually a scene where the nemesis lusts after the hero's gift. The nemesis sees it as their birthright and wants the powers so they can rule the world and do evil things. The hero always has a formidable enemy that wants him destroyed.

Similarly, Jesus not only had Satan to contend with, but He also had those who were afraid of change, who wanted to keep control of the religious people, or who were threatened in some way by Jesus. This is easily seen when He released his superpower—and I'm not talking about healing people, casting out demons, feeding the multitudes, or walking on water. I'm talking about something that pushed the buttons of the religious nemeses of Jesus so much. It not only made them angry at Jesus, it made them want to kill Him. Let us go to a day in the life of Jesus and see for ourselves.

> *A few days later, when Jesus again entered Capernaum, the people heard that He had come home. They gathered in such large numbers that there was no room left, not even outside the door, and He preached the word to them. Some men came, bringing to Him a paralyzed man, carried by four of them. Since they could not get him to Jesus because of the crowd, they made an opening in the roof above Jesus by digging through it and then lowered the mat the man was lying on. When*

Jesus saw their faith, He said to the paralyzed man, "Son, your sins are forgiven."

Now some teachers of the law were sitting there, thinking to themselves, "Why does this fellow talk like that? He's blaspheming! Who can forgive sins but God alone?"

Immediately Jesus knew in his spirit that this was what they were thinking in their hearts, and He said to them, "Why are you thinking these things? Which is easier: to say to this paralyzed man, 'Your sins are forgiven,' or to say, 'Get up, take your mat and walk'? But I want you to know that the Son of Man has authority on earth to forgive sins." So He said to the man, "I tell you, get up, take your mat and go home." He got up, took his mat and walked out in full view of them all. This amazed everyone and they praised God, saying, "We have never seen anything like this!"
(Mark 2:1–12)

I love this story because it illustrates so much. We could camp out here for a long time. Completely ignoring that the man was supernaturally healed, the religious people focused instead on what Jesus said. Jesus released His superpower to forgive sins and explained to them He did it so they would know that He had the authority to forgive sins on earth.

This was a big deal, bigger than you may think. To be fair to the religious people of that day, we must provide some context. If they sinned one way or another, there was a code of law dictating specifically what they had to sacrifice in the presence of a priest in order to be forgiven. Many of their sacrifices involved the killing of a real-life, breathing animal, and they had to watch it being killed right in front of them because of what they had done. The high priest would kill a spotless lamb for the sins of the people. Sin was serious business for the Jewish people of that day.

When Jesus used His superpower of forgiving sin on the spot without a sacrifice or investigation by just saying, "Your sins are forgiven," this was a world-changing event. The leaders were right in claiming only God could do that, but they couldn't see that He was right in front of them.

Jesus also demonstrated His superpower to forgive sins toward a woman with a past in Luke 7.

> *When one of the Pharisees invited Jesus to have dinner with him, He went to the Pharisee's house and reclined at the table. A woman in that town who lived a sinful life learned that Jesus was eating at the Pharisee's house, so she came there with an alabaster jar of perfume. As*

she stood behind him at His feet weeping, she began to wet His feet with her tears. Then she wiped them with her hair, kissed them and poured perfume on them.

When the Pharisee who had invited him saw this, he said to himself, "If this man were a prophet, he would know who is touching him and what kind of woman she is—that she is a sinner."

Jesus answered him, "Simon, I have something to tell you."

"Tell me, teacher," he said.

"Two people owed money to a certain moneylender. One owed him five hundred denarii, and the other fifty. Neither of them had the money to pay him back, so He forgave the debts of both. Now, which of them will love him more?"

Simon replied, "I suppose the one who had the bigger debt forgiven."

"You have judged correctly," Jesus said.

Then He turned toward the woman and said to Simon, "Do you see this woman? I came into your house. You did not give me any water for my feet, but she wet my feet with her tears and wiped them with her hair. You did not give me a kiss, but this woman, from the time I entered, has not stopped kissing my feet. You did not put oil on my head, but she has poured perfume on my feet. Therefore, I tell you, her many sins have been forgiven—as her great love has shown. But whoever has been forgiven little loves little."

Then Jesus said to her, "Your sins are forgiven."

The other guests began to say among themselves, "Who is this who even forgives sins?"

Jesus said to the woman, "Your faith has saved you; go in peace" (Luke 7:36–50)

Forgiving a sinful woman like that must have been quite the scene at the dinner table. This was unheard of at that time, and again, the Pharisees were more focused on what Jesus said rather than the woman who had been freed from a tainted past. This new superpower of Jesus was raising eyebrows and some deep concerns. God was doing something revolutionary—He was forgiving sins.

This was a mind-blowing concept then and is still mind-blowing today. Think of it. To be completely forgiven of your sins by simply asking for them to be forgiven and receiving the sacrifice of Christ. I love how Paul put it: *"And you, being dead in your sins and the uncircumcision of your flesh, hath He quickened together with him, having forgiven you all trespasses"* (Colossians 2:13 KJV).

Our Turn

This mind-blowing, change-the-world superpower that Christ had is now ours in Him. Jesus died to give us His powers to do many things, and forgiving sins is one of them. We'll get much more into this by another campfire on our hike, but for now, I just want to whet your appetite for activating your superpower. It's like a coach motivating you to envision how to play a particular sport by opening your mind and heart to the possibility of using your athleticism so that you not only become successful but also win that big championship or gold medal.

As I shared with you earlier on our journey, I have lived in Colorado Springs for over twenty years. There are many striking things about this city. There's the majestic Garden of the Gods park, which is only a couple of miles from my office. Towering in the background is Pikes Peak, a 14,115-foot, often snowcapped mountain visible from every location in the city. However, there is something else Colorado Springs is well known for. We are called the Olympic City because the US Olympic & Paralympic Training Center is located here. World-class athletes, both male and female, move here from all over the country to train for their particular sport. When I say *train*, I mean they spend countless hours a day studying the winning techniques of their event, stretching, working out, and getting their nutrition in order. Like the heroes in our movies, they are in that training and mastering of their gift part of the story. That is what you are about to enter in the chapters ahead.

Christ has paid for and given you the supernatural ability to forgive sins. This is an exciting gift to have; however, we need to practice and train ourselves to be able to forgive sin. *"Have nothing to do with godless myths and old wives' tales,"* wrote Paul, *"rather, train yourself to be godly"* (1 Timothy 4:7). There are many aspects to godliness. Forgiveness is one, and it requires training. Training is a biblical concept.

A few decades back, MercyMe released their song "I Can Only Imagine," which captured the hearts of the world. I want your heart to be captured as you begin to imagine the freedom and peace you will experience as you come to realize the complete forgiveness of all the sins you have committed, both great and small, past and present. How would you feel to have that load of guilt and shame lifted off your shoulders, never to have to carry again? Imagine running full speed toward your spiritual destiny with no sense of any chains from your past. Imagine your smile as you wake up in the mornings, covered in the secure blanket of total forgiveness, not only by the Father but by yourself. You are no longer keeping a record of your past wrongs because, as 1 Corinthians 13:5 says, *"[Love] keeps no record of wrongs."* This is your life every day.

Now imagine being able to go down the corridor of those who have sinned against you—that person, that event—and then being able to forgive from your heart, not just your mind, totally freeing you. Imagine being freed from the knots in your gut when they are mentioned in a conversation, or seeing a scene in a movie and not feeling triggered or not going back to that dark or ashamed place. Imagine being more free than you have ever been. You're no longer looking over your proverbial shoulder but looking forward. Imagine the clarity of your heart and mind that are no longer tainted or afraid of facing anyone from the past. Imagine the confidence you could have as you develop your superpower of Forgiveness for Everyone, as you walk into a future where there is most likely a guarantee that you will sin and that others will sin against you. Instead of it being like a bullet that takes you out for a while, you can be like the character Wolverine in the X-Men movies and spit that bullet out, go about your life with family and friends, and follow Christ with all your heart.

I'm not talking hyperbole here. I am talking from my personal experience of being empowered to forgive fathers who never showed up, of forgiving those who sexually abused, neglected, were responsible for getting us addicted to something, and otherwise hurt us. I know sin, and by the grace of God, I know the forgiveness of sin. It reminds me of the quote "I have been poor, and I have been rich. Rich is better." I have been stuck with not knowing how to forgive others or myself or even truly experience the forgiveness of Christ in my heart, and then growing to be able to forgive them, me, and receive the Father's forgiveness. I can personally attest that the latter is SOOO much better!

I didn't realize how potent this superpower was until I kept growing in influence and leadership in the body of Christ and began experiencing firsthand being attacked, lied about, and sinned against. But like Wolverine, I now can chuck those bullets out of my system as fast as they come in, and those sad people are in no way able to absorb my time or gain control of my steering wheel.

Forgiveness for Everyone is like strengthening a muscle or stretching one, depending on your age. At first, it seems challenging; however, as you practice, you get stronger and more flexible. After developing the tools that I am going to give you and having you practice forgiving others, regardless of how difficult it might feel now, I guarantee it will become easier in the future.

As we continue our journey, you will truly be amazed at how able you can be to forgive others and yourself, and to fully accept the Lord's forgiveness. When Jesus hung on the cross for us, He cried, *"It is finished"* (John 19:30). He meant it.

So, we are at that part of the journey where we take the "before" picture. You know, the one before everyone has started to sweat or be challenged or wish they hadn't done this hike yet. You can, in your mind, take a picture of yourself or actually take out that cell phone and snap a close-up picture of your face, capturing your eyes.

I have seen that those who do the work that's ahead look different in their face and eyes. Their countenance is brighter, and their eyes reflect the difference this journey makes in their life. It's because so much of the toxic stuff weighing them down is gone, and they start perceiving life much differently and more positively than prior to taking this journey.

Keep this snapshot, and when you're done doing all the work, take the second one and send it to my office at Heart to Heart Counseling Center at heart2heart@xc.org. We love seeing the smiles of those who have taken the journey. Of course, everything is confidential. We will just smile and be proud of your accomplishment. It can be done!

You Don't Have to Be Jesus

I wouldn't be a proper guide if I didn't tell a real story about someone who was able to use their superpower with excellence. I do this to inspire you because, occasionally, I get some resistance to the idea that we can forgive everyone. The Christian version of this resistance is, "Dr. Doug, you know I am not Jesus. I mean, I'm glad He could do it, but let's be real. I'm not Him."

When that happens I just relax, smile, and say, "If I can tell you a true story of incredible forgiveness, would you reconsider trying?" They usually are willing to listen, but in their heart of hearts, they really don't believe any story could inspire them to let go of the things they are holding on to. They, of course, are expecting me to tell them a story of a man being beaten so badly he was hospitalized, a person who saw their parents shot in front of them, a woman who was sexually abused for decades or sold into a sex trade. Although those stories about forgiveness are amazing, that's not the story I choose.

At that, I pick up my phone from my desk and hit my YouVersion Bible App. You should see the looks on their faces, which might be just about how you might be feeling. *What is Dr. Weiss going to pull out of his pocket now?* they seem to be wondering. I open the book of Acts and read this portion found in Acts 6 and 7. Let's start with chapter 6.

> *"Now Stephen, a man full of God's grace and power, performed great wonders and signs among the people. Opposition arose, however, from members of the Synagogue of the Freedmen (as it was called)—Jews of Cyrene and Alexandria as well as the provinces of Cilicia and Asia—who began to argue with Stephen. But they could not stand up against the wisdom the Spirit gave him as he spoke.*
>
> *Then they secretly persuaded some men to say, "We have heard Stephen speak blasphemous words against Moses and against God."*
>
> *So they stirred up the people and the elders and the teachers of the law. They seized Stephen and brought him before the Sanhedrin. They produced false witnesses, who testified, "This fellow never stops speaking against this holy place and against the law. For we have heard him say that this Jesus of Nazareth will*

> *destroy this place and change the customs Moses handed down to us."*
>
> *All who were sitting in the Sanhedrin looked intently at Stephen, and they saw that his face was like the face of an angel."* (Acts 6:8–15)

Here we see Stephen was not only a deacon, he was manifesting signs and wonders just like the apostles. He was being persecuted for the miracles, and the religious people wanted to stop this because the church was gaining influence and prosperity. They most likely felt both incompetent and threatened by Stephen, which can be a lethal combination.

Stephen was falsely charged and then gave one of the most concise history lessons to his accusers, which you can read at the beginning of chapter 7. It was so convicting that they had an evil response. Stephen continues:

> *"You stiff-necked people! Your hearts and ears are still uncircumcised. You are just like your ancestors: You always resist the Holy Spirit! Was there ever a prophet your ancestors did not persecute? They even killed those who predicted the coming of the Righteous One. And now you have betrayed and murdered him—you who*

have received the law that was given through angels but have not obeyed it."

When the members of the Sanhedrin heard this, they were furious and gnashed their teeth at him. But Stephen, full of the Holy Spirit, looked up to heaven and saw the glory of God, and Jesus standing at the right hand of God. "Look," he said, "I see heaven open and the Son of Man standing at the right hand of God."

At this they covered their ears and, yelling at the top of their voices, they all rushed at him, dragged him out of the city and began to stone him. Meanwhile, the witnesses laid their coats at the feet of a young man named Saul.

While they were stoning him, Stephen prayed, "Lord Jesus, receive my spirit." Then he fell on his knees and cried out, "Lord, do not hold this sin against them." When he had said this, he fell asleep." (Acts 7:51–60)

There is so much here we could unpack for hours, but I want to stay on our path. Here it is: Stephen was literally being stoned to death. Imagine the horror. He was thrown to the ground by people he knew and had possibly grown up with. These same people were now throwing rock after rock at his body and head with the absolute intent to snuff out his life.

Yet, while the stones were pelting him, causing great pain, instead of responding with anger and condemnation, Stephen looked to heaven and made a profound statement of forgiveness. "Lord," he cried out, "don't hold this sin against them." The statement echoes Jesus crying out, *"Father, forgive them, for they know not what they do"* (Luke 23:34 ESV). Stephen not only knew the Lord intimately, he knew how to use this superpower we have been discussing.

There is one more important point in this scene. Throughout the epistles, there are several references to Christ sitting at the right hand of God. However, here, Stephen saw Jesus *standing* at the right hand of God. It's as if Jesus was giving Stephen a standing ovation, not only for being a martyr but also for using his superpower as he breathed his last breath, just as Jesus Himself did on the cross. What a beautiful sight to have done something that caused heaven to not only notice but to stand in awe itself. You, too, can be a Stephen and take this journey of Forgiveness for Everyone. You can please Jesus as He watches His nature pouring through you in the process.

CHAPTER FIVE

Me

One of the greatest perks of long hikes, especially those all-day excursions, is you know you are going to get to take an occasional rest. Almost every trail I have ever hiked has natural places for a small group to stop and let their bodies and souls regroup. These areas are usually right along the trail, and the guide knows where they are located. He will actually plan the hike in advance and set the pace in accordance with the resting spots. This is critical because of a couple of things. First, as you climb, it requires more and more effort for the muscles in your body to meet the incline demands of the mountain. Second, the higher the altitude you ascend to, the thinner the air gets, giving you less and less oxygen to do the task of climbing. Breathing becomes heavier and increasing fatigue also makes your entire body feel sluggish.

These mountain resting spots, created by God, typically have big rocks or boulders that are softer than you may think and are heated by the sun. They are nature's way of offering support and protection to the weary traveler. Surprising and wonderful things happen on hikes when you sit down to let your body regroup. A deer or squirrel may meander right up to you. You may find yourself relaxing beside a trickling creek or river, where the sound is like God singing you into a tranquil place of peace. You just might take a nap. Another added benefit when you sit with your friends, family, or even strangers that you've been hiking with is that you often start engaging in meaningful dialogue. It seems sitting around with others on big rocks surrounded by breathtaking scenery has a way of opening us up. Maybe it's the psychologist in me, but when I'm mountain climbing with a group, I love it when the time comes for us to sit around and have those little chats. So, at this spot on our journey of forgiving everyone, I thought it would be an ideal place for us to just sit and talk a bit. And this will probably be one of the more important chats we will have.

One Monday morning, I started counseling a couple who'd flown in all the way from Switzerland for a weeklong marriage intensive. That's how desperate they were. The husband, Drake, was a wealthy entrepreneur. Both he and his wife, Jacqueline, were in their mid-fifties and dressed to the nines. Their image projected, "We've got it together," yet if you peered behind their longing eyes, it wouldn't take a counselor to see their lives were anything but together. Their marriage was on the rocks because Drake had been intentionally withholding spiritual, emotional, and sexual intimacy from Jacqueline for over two decades, leaving her in great pain and insecure about her personal worth. To start the sessions, I took the couple through my normal evaluation of their intake process. Immediately, the red lights started flashing. Sure enough, Drake fit all the criteria for Intimacy Anorexia. Since they had not had sex in over seven years, he took a polygraph to verify he had not cheated on her. Fortunately, he passed. Next, I met with Jacqueline alone, listening to her story and feelings. After that, I met with Drake to learn what caused the intimacy anorexia he had. It came as no surprise to discover that throughout his life, Drake had a regular porn and self-behavior problem. This itself could be a cause, but he also had an emotionally distant and cold mother from whom he had been detached since early childhood. On top of that, growing up in an overly strict, religious household with a dad who served on the church board, he was expected to be a really "good boy"—or else.

After going off to college, Drake shook off the chains of his parents' constraints and experimented with alcohol, some drugs, and women. During his first semester, he also had his first sexual encounter, and wouldn't you know it, the girl got pregnant. They agreed to have an abortion, which Drake paid for. The following semester, she moved to another college, and the relationship fizzled. Two years later, he met his wife, Jacqueline.

In our sessions, we addressed Drake's mother, father, and the church, his on-and-off struggle with porn, and his behavior issues. All of which he was ready and willing to address. Then, I had him begin working through an exercise that helps a person determine if they have truly forgiven themselves. I'll show you the exercise shortly. Drake didn't have too much of a problem forgiving himself for his early behaviors and even some of the significant things he had done during his marriage. However, when it came to the abortion, he locked up so tight that he couldn't speak or move for minutes. Finally, Drake squeaked, "I can't do it, Doc. Can't do it!" As the words spilled out of his mouth, his face contorted, revealing the pure torture he was experiencing while reliving that part of his story.

As the week went on, Drake was able to forgive himself completely and restore his marriage, as so many couples do during an intensive. He got a handle on his porn problem, and after seven long years of detachment, intimacy with his wife returned.

There's an important reason I shared Drake's story with you as we chat on the warm mountain rocks here at our resting spot. One of the most difficult things to do is forgive yourself. For years, I've watched client after client struggle with this. Even if the person has suffered greatly at the hands of others, they still feel guilty, like it's their fault. They repeatedly tell me that forgiving themselves was much harder than forgiving those who wounded them. It's not an overreach to say I've heard this more than a few thousand times from every type of person you can imagine.

Sinning Against Ourselves

I can't remember ever hearing a sermon in church or being taught in Sunday school on how we actually sin against ourselves, and then how we can forgive ourselves for those sins. I will explain this process in detail in a future segment. Oh, we've been taught consistently and fervently how we sin against God and others and the church, but rarely, if ever, are we taught that we sin against ourselves. In some religious circles, it would be considered selfish and even sinful to think of such. You must take the focus off yourself and die to yourself, they say. Yet forgiving yourself and releasing the load of guilt you've been carrying, even from sinning against yourself, doesn't mean you are self-centered. I know that's a lot of "ourselves" and "yourselves" and "themselves." It's because the points in this chapter are foundational to your ultimate freedom.

Think about it. Out of all the sermons you've sat through and listened to, and of all the Christian books you've read, how many taught that when you sin, you sin against yourself? I've been a Christian for over forty years and can confidently say that I have never, ever heard a sermon that addresses sinning against myself. However, when we sin, that's precisely what we are doing because we are going against our God-given design. We get knotted up inside with reoccurring thoughts and memories of our sins that can torture us, even on our "good" days. These thoughts of self-condemnation can spiral us into incredible sorrow. It's common for me to counsel people who are living in emotional turmoil because they have connected the dots of some current negative event to their past sins and mistakes. They believe God is punishing them now for something they did years earlier. That's what Donna did.

Donna was a professional who had seen considerable success in her real estate career. She came to see me because of issues in her marriage. Just as I would do with any couple on the Monday of a five-day intensive, I began by going through her story. I asked the standard questions about her family of origin, if there was any depression or neglect, her sexual history, and so forth. Then, I asked her one specific question. Years ago, I learned from experience that when asking a woman about her history, I would make sure to ask: "Have you ever had an abortion?" (In the case of a male client, the question is: "Have you ever taken part in an abortion?")

Donna was stunned by the question. It was like I had hit her in the head with a two-by-four. As with most women (or men) in counseling, she had never been asked this directly. Since she was a believer and lying wasn't an option, she dropped her head and admitted that, yes, abortion was indeed part of her past. When Donna was only sixteen, she got pregnant by a pastor's son whom she dated in high school. He was older than her and on his way to college when she found out. In panic and desperation, she located a clinic where they comforted her and promised to take care of the "problem," and assured her she would be fine. However, instead of being free like she thought she'd be, a dark cloud of sadness and regret followed her from that point on. We are as sick as our secrets and our unforgiveness. Donna's personality changed because of hers.

As we dove deeper into her history, Donna told me that later on, after she was married and really wanted to get pregnant, she was unable. This went on for quite some time. Finally, conception happened, but the joy was short-lived when it was discovered that she had a blighted ovum, which meant there was no embryo in her sac. In her grieving state, Donna believed wholeheartedly that it was God's judgment for her abortion, which she felt was an unforgivable sin. In her head, she knew Jesus had forgiven her, but she never could forgive herself.

Seasons of self-loathing haunted her until she did what I will share with you later. The truth is, Donna's blighted ovum had nothing to do with God's punishment. Statistics confirm that it happens about 50 percent of the time with natural miscarriages that occur in the first few months of pregnancy. It usually only happens once, and most women go on to bear children. After this experience, Donna eventually gave birth to three healthy girls. Yet, she continued to carry the load of unforgiveness toward herself. She worked through the exercises found in *Finding Grace After Abortion*,[2] and eventually, she was not only able to forgive herself but also to be free from the effects of the abortion.

Donna's experience of wrongfully connecting the dots of some sin in her past to a present trauma is common. The Enemy of our souls wants us to walk in condemnation. The Bible calls him the *"accuser of our brethren"* (Revelation 12:10 KJV). It's not that we are not guilty of sin. Sin is missing the mark of God's best and is not to be taken lightly. *"For the wages of sin is death"* (Romans 6:23 KJV), wrote Paul. There are serious consequences to sin, both spiritual and physical. Yet, God made a way for us. Paul continued, *"But the gift of God is eternal life through Jesus Christ our Lord"* (Romans 6:23 KJV). The accuser comes in after we have sought forgiveness and received God's gift through Jesus. He relentlessly makes accusations against those trusting God's provision for forgiveness, reminding them of their past weaknesses, sins, and failures. The goal is to get them to doubt that they are forgiven or can be forgiven and render their lives ineffective. Satan is not only an accuser, he's also a thief and a liar seeking to steal our life by using his lies (John 10:10, 8:44).

All of us sin, and when we do, it leaves a crack that must be filled not only by *God's* grace and forgiveness but also by *our own* grace and forgiveness for ourselves. If our cracks are not filled by these two sources, we will experience self-condemnation, false guilt, or shame, sometimes for decades on end. I have met many who've had so much self-condemnation that they felt disqualified from any service to Christ. As a result, they sit in church absorbing but not serving because of that feeling of uncleanness that comes from not forgiving themselves. When God forgives us, and we forgive ourselves, we are free to forgive and love others in different ways.

I have seen thousands of souls who have never considered that when they sin, they are sinning against themselves and hurting their own spirit, soul, and body. Some of these souls hide in secret for decades as they medicate with carbs, sugar, caffeine, nicotine, pornography, video games, entertainment, workaholism—you name it. The price they pay for not forgiving themselves and then self-medicating is incalculable. It's especially heartbreaking because they could have been free years earlier if they'd only had the tools and understanding to use their superpower of forgiving sin on themselves. So many Christians struggle by not giving grace and unconditional forgiveness toward their own souls.

I've known both men and women who have suffered needlessly from depression, trying to suppress some secret sin, or have lived in agonizing anxiety for fear that their secret sin would be exposed, rendering them permanently unlovable. When we choose to cover our sins or stand in unforgiveness toward ourselves, we can morph in so many unhealthy ways. Some become hyper-religious and able to quote scripture after scripture ad nauseam, yet have zero grace for others or themselves. When they do finally experience authentic forgiveness of their own sin from God and themselves, they are magnificently transformed into people of mercy, patience, and compassion. I've seen it happen again and again. Instead of emitting that religious, judgmental stench, there's a fragrance of humility and grace on them. It's the scent of Jesus.

In the Forgiveness for Everyone process, you are going to start grasping what it really means to forgive all people, including the person staring back at you in the mirror. That soul is worthy of being forgiven by you as well. Consistently, over the years, clients have come back to me after their intensives and have said that forgiving themselves was one of the most profoundly liberating and healing experiences of their lives. I agree. I'll never forget doing this exercise on myself, and that feeling when the burden of my own sin that I'd been carrying for so many years was lifted. The lightness, the joy, the freedom! Not freedom to sin, but freedom from sin, freedom to live, and love for the Lord. *"For my yoke is easy and my burden is light"* (Matthew 11:30), said Jesus. I found out it's true and haven't carried that burden since. I was close to thirty at that time and had been a Christian for over a decade. I'd even gone to

Bible school and seminary. Yet, not once during all those years was I taught how to take practical steps to forgive not only what I had done to others but what I had done to myself—body, soul, and spirit.

Regarding how sin and unforgiveness affect our physical bodies, I should take a side trail for a moment on that alone. When we sin, our mind holds the memory of what occurred. What we don't realize, however, is how often our body holds the memory too. This is especially true when it comes to sexual sin. Let me explain.

1 Corinthians 6:18 says, *"Flee from sexual immorality. All other sins a person commits are outside the body, but whoever sins sexually, sins against their own body."* I remember reading this in my Bible school days, and it hit me like a lightning rod. Up to that point, I had been taught that all sins were equal, yet here I was reading a scripture that directly opposed that notion. I asked my professors why this sin was different. They had no answers and blew me off. When I graduated from Bible school and moved on to seminary, I was sure my professors there would be able to help me solve this dilemma. Looking back, I now know it was the Holy Spirit who kept it in my mind for so long because He knew the answer would be critical to my calling. So, I asked my philosophy professor and theology professor, who were both brilliant men. Neither had any answer as to why

sexual sin is different and why it impacts the physical body. In the end, none of my professors could help me.

Around the same time that I graduated and went into private practice, the field of neuropsychology was really starting to take off. In short, neuropsychology is the study of how the brain interacts with the nervous system and how those interactions affect the body, behavior, and cognition. I started following this field, and it led me to the answer I was looking for regarding 1 Corinthians 6:18. I go into great detail on this in my book *Sex, Men and God*,[3] but I am going to give you the elevator version as we rest here in our mountain paradise together.

When we have an orgasm with a real person, a fantasy person, or a pornographic image, there is a release of the highest level of pleasure brain chemicals our body can naturally produce. When a person experiences an orgasm, their whole brain lights up. Whatever you are looking at during that moment of chemical release, real or imagined, your brain literally glues to the image and will want whatever or whoever that is again and again. This is all part of God's design so that when we become one within marriage, we are strongly attached in a neurological manner. That's why after fifty years of marriage, a man can say he is so attracted to his wife. There has been nearly a lifetime of neuro conditioning.

On the negative side, when someone connects neurologically to images or people prior to or outside of marriage, it can create physical appetites that are destructive, yet they will still crave them.

Remember the study of Pavlov's dogs? Pavlov combined the sound of a bell with the offering of food. Eventually, the dogs associated the bell with food and began to salivate at the sound of the bell, even when no food was given. That's how we are designed sexually and what makes sexual sin different. This is why it's harder for a couple to break up if they have been having sex. We neurologically feel what the scripture says: "... *and the two shall become one flesh*" (Matthew 19:5 NKJV). When one flesh tears apart, an emotional ripping takes place down to the neurological elements of our being.

I share this because many of us have had these experiences, and there was a tearing and ripping that has left neurological and emotional wounds that, in many cases, are still sore or festering many years later. We have to be intentional about forgiving some of these relationships and forgiving ourselves for our role. Sex, when it is a sin, is not unforgivable by God. The guilt or shame associated with it can not only be forgiven by God but must be forgiven by us too. When we do forgive ourselves, the burden from those youthful chapters or adult mistakes is lifted, and we can walk in the freedom Christ has purchased for us. I had to forgive myself for a lot here, and I have been free from those mistakes for decades.

These mistakes or sins in no way change the gifts and callings of God in your life. Romans 11:29 makes this very clear: *"For the gifts and calling of God are irrevocable"* (NKJV). Here is how I have explained this to my clients, especially those who have been in various Christian leadership roles. When God created you, He gave you your DNA on every level—skills, talents, intelligence, and the abilities and calling to fulfill His purposes for your life.

I must remind you that He never designed you for what you may think you are made for. A pine seed from a pine cone can struggle and wish and work hard and even pray to be an oak tree, but it will always be a pine because that's how it was designed from conception. We all started as a seed from our parents with our unique DNA. Unlike plants and animals, however, man was created in the image of God and made to connect with Him through relationship. After the fall, that connection was disrupted because of sin and must be reconnected through His provision of forgiveness. Once we are returned to right relationship with Him and the connection restored, we come back into alignment with how we were designed. He then leads and guides us with excellence to fulfill His mission for our lives. The seed that is us from the beginning will become what God wanted it to become as we follow Him. Regardless of how lost we get or how much we sin, we will always be our seed.

As I shared earlier, Heart to Heart Counseling Center is located in Colorado Springs, and in my personal office there, I have a huge window with views of the mountain peaks. It's stunning, and sometimes I have to pinch myself to see if it's real or a dream. I feel so blessed. Outside the window are two huge trees that deer are fond of and occasionally rest beneath. Often, I ask my clients if they see those trees out my window. They say yes, of course, because it's kind of hard to miss them. I say, "You know something about those trees? They will always be trees. They may want to be a flower or a bush or a race car, but they will always be a tree because God made them a tree. Now, regardless of how hard it rains, how cold it gets, how much snow their branches carry in the winter, or how hot it gets in the summer, they will still be trees. And they will also be 'that' particular kind of tree because that's the type of seed they came from."

The point is this: It doesn't matter what storms you have gone through, nor does it matter whether you or others have created the storm. You are still a tree and a particular type of tree, so to speak. Nothing, and I mean nothing, disqualifies you from God's design for you. You might have delays, but you can still have the fruit in your life if you plant by the living water to become the life-giving person you are supposed to be. This is one of the greatest perks of living a lifestyle of Forgiveness for Everyone. You get to become the best version of God's design for your life, and a blessing to those who watch your tree grow to become what it is to become, providing comforting shade and resources for others.

Okay, after that important side trail, let's get back to the path, shall we? It's true, we all not only sin against God and others, but also against ourselves. We know the harmful things that we *shouldn't* do, yet we do them anyway, resulting in self-inflicted wounds to our hearts. On the other hand, we know the right things we *should* do and find ourselves not doing them. So, we sin against ourselves, and this sin grows like an unseen plague in our lives. This plague, over time, can become regret for lost opportunities. When we don't forgive ourselves, we can experience negative symptoms from not doing this work. I want to share some of those symptoms I have seen sitting in the chair across from me with different faces, genders, ages, and religions. These symptoms of not forgiving ourselves seem to be somewhat universal.

Symptoms of Not Forgiving Yourself

1. We have a lower opinion of ourselves. I have seen people feel so worthless because they are holding on to their sins against themselves. If this is you, and you still struggle even after doing the Forgiveness for Everyone piece, I would dig deep into the *Worthy* series[4] to specifically get rid of any trace of worthlessness in your life. You are worth the blood of Christ because He says so. *"For our sake he made Him to be sin who knew no sin so that in Him we might become the righteousness of God"* (2 Corinthians 5:21 ESV). We are worthy because Christ took our place and made us worthy, *"giving thanks unto the Father, who has made us worthy to participate in the inheritance of the saints in light"* (Colossians 1:12 JUB). I'll never forget when He told me this early in my walk with Him, and I have not struggled with it since. You heard my story, so you know I had plenty to feel worthless about.
2. We can extend grace to others but not to ourselves. This has always been fascinating to me. A person could have several severe perpetrators and, after doing the exercise, could forgive them

all. Yet when it came to themselves, they would have to really work through it a few times until they finally granted forgiveness to themselves.

3. We struggle with the whole idea of even God or others forgiving us. When we don't forgive ourselves, sometimes we struggle with the entire idea that Jesus really forgives us. We may cognitively tell ourselves that He does, but experientially, we don't believe it, feel it, or behave as if we are truly forgiven.

4. We create a system of punishment or penitence for ourselves. This is unique to some. They might deny themselves pleasures and relationships or not reach for goals and sabotage successful relationships. There is no need to ever try to pay for our sins because they have been paid for, and we have been given the superpower of forgiving sins, even our own sins.

5. We don't really believe we should live a blessed life. This goes with the sabotaging, but it's more internal. As we prosper, our families grow healthy, and life is good, there is an internal gnawing that we shouldn't have it this good because of what we did in our past.

6. We struggle with shame. We tell ourselves, *If people really knew my secrets, they wouldn't love*

me. This core belief causes you to block the flow of love being given to you, even from your spouse. This can also allow you to justify sabotaging or addictive behaviors. Most addicts have this belief because of the secrets they keep and their inability to forgive themselves.

7. We don't get too close to people out of fear they will find out we are imperfect. Spoiler alert here: they already know that we are imperfect! This keeping our walls up even to our family and spouse keeps us from receiving and enjoying love.

8. We keep track of our sins and are way more able to tell ourselves what is wrong with us than what is right with us. I can't tell you how many clients I have asked the question, "What's right about you?" or "What is wonderful about you?" And they look at me, as they say in Texas, "like a cow staring at a new gate." It's a real challenge for them to articulate any positive attributes about themselves. Sometimes, I have to leave the room for a while and wait until they can turn the gear in their thinking enough to write down ten encouraging things about themselves.

9. We hide in addictions like work, food, porn, and social media. Addictions are common for

those who don't forgive themselves. The addiction serves to escape or medicate the past. If you have tried to stop, promised yourself and others you were going to stop, had consequences, haven't feel good without the behavior or substance, and it has decreased positive activities in your life, you might have an addiction. I would recommend my book that you read my book *Recovery for Everyone*[5] and get in some sort of accountability relationship or group to heal this addiction issue.

10. We don't look people in the eye or let people look us in the eye. I find people who struggle with forgiving themselves have challenges with prolonged eye contact. By prolonged, I mean from fifteen seconds to a minute. I have had to do an eye-gazing exercise where a couple looks into each other's eyes for the first fifteen seconds, then thirty, working up to two full minutes. This is to be able to reset the person and their brain to be present with their spouse. Try it. It's harder than you think, especially if you are stuck somewhere in your soul.

11. We won't take risks. This could be risking our hearts in relationships by being truly transparent, or risking being honest about ourselves

and admitting when we are wrong. The risk could also be in our careers or businesses, or serving in ministry, and so on.

12. Our narrative in our head about us is slanted in the negative direction. Only you can know if the voice about you that rolls around is mostly cheerleader or critic. How we think about ourselves internally will impact our external life in some way, for sure.

13. We are critical of ourselves, and this criticism expands to others as well. I think criticism is a "friend" that people utilize so they don't have to trust in relationships. Let's face it, we all are imperfect sinners and sometimes self-willed, selfish, or simply not fun to be around. That should not disqualify us from being able to see the best in others and have healthy relationships.

14. We make bad relationship choices because we don't feel worthy. This is something I have seen more with women, but I've seen it with men as well. They pick people with low self-esteem, anger, and addictions—people who are generally immature or lazy with a limited capacity to love. They do this throughout their lives, usually because of their feelings of worthlessness.

As you forgive yourself, you feel better about yourself and want to care and protect yourself in healthy ways, so your relationships go through a change as well.

15. We have trouble with boundaries. This can go in both directions. You can be so rigid that hardly anyone qualifies to get inside your heart. The other way is you have such poor boundaries that you can't say no, and everyone has more value than you. You might justify this to yourself as being sacrificial, but others would see you as being a doormat unnecessarily.

16. We want to project a perfect image so nobody questions us. This false front is super at everything, super Christian, financially great, and dresses perfectly. You know the type. They look so good nobody would ever question that they struggle with self-forgiveness or anything else.

17. We have a challenge admitting we were wrong. This is so common with those who struggle to forgive themselves. If they make a mistake, they are all bad and unlovable. If they are imperfect, they need a video to prove they are wrong. This is not fun to live with because then you are always the problem or wrong because they find it so difficult to be flawed and loved.

18. We get caught up in wanting others to approve of us because we don't. The need for personal or professional adoration can become excessive due to the hole in our soul from not being able to forgive ourselves. You might not be as aware of this, but consider looking at how often you seek credit for things or wanting to be appreciated on a regular basis that seems maybe needy to others.

When we don't forgive ourselves, we can get into all sorts of internal conundrums. However, once you forgive yourself, it's like this big ball of yarn begins to unravel, and you can live life in a totally different way. I have experienced both, and forgiving yourself is a better way to live.

Benefits of Forgiving Yourself

1. We have a more balanced opinion of ourselves and believe that we are flawed *and* loved, not flawed *or* loved. This is a huge difference.
2. We extend grace to ourselves because we accept that we will, at times, need it. This becomes easier and easier over time as you practice your superpower of forgiving sins.

3. We no longer struggle with the whole idea of God or others forgiving us and accepting that they can and do forgive us. Letting this into our hearts is truly liberating and life-changing.
4. We accept grace and don't try to earn it in any way from God or others who extend it toward us.
5. We really believe we can live a blessed life and enjoy the blessings of God from a place of gratitude.
6. We don't struggle with shame. We think to ourselves, *If people really knew my secrets, they wouldn't love me.* We are past being secret keepers and protecting our secrets, and we live transparently.
7. We get close to people and let them find out we are imperfect and loved. Of course, we are using wisdom, but it feels great to have some friends.
8. We stop keeping track of our sins and are actually able to accept compliments from strangers, friends, and even our family.
9. We desire and can heal from addictions like work, food, porn, social media, or other self-destructive behaviors that are limiting us in some manner. We accept this path because we are worthy of the best life possible.

10. We look people in the eye or let people look us in the eye. We feel more connected to people. We are being seen and seeing others at a deeper level.
11. We take risks personally and professionally in our intimate relationships and even in our recreation.
12. Our narrative in our head about ourselves is more balanced. The negative noise is in the distant past.
13. We are much less critical of ourselves and others. We see the strengths of ourselves and others.
14. We make better relationship choices because we feel worthy of good relationships. This takes a while, but I have seen people re-landscape their relationships with people who honor them in a relationship.
15. We have healthy boundaries.
16. We are authentic and do not create an image of ourselves that we must manage or protect.
17. We admit when we are wrong without even being asked, even if others would not have found out about it. We are comfortable that, as imperfect creatures, we goof and miss it at times.
18. Trusting good people becomes easier and more common in our lives.
19. We don't get caught up in wanting others to approve of us.

Living in a state of forgiving yourself is so freeing. I describe it as being able to breathe after you have a cold. You have a new lease on life, and you are just lighter, able to be more present with others, and you seem to have more energy for life.

You can decide which list applies to you. Know your goal as you move through doing Forgiveness for Everyone, and hopefully, you will experience these symptoms for the rest of your life.

CHAPTER SIX

First Things First

Earlier in our journey, I shared with you that Colorado Springs is home to the US Olympic & Paralympic Training Center. There are a lot of elite athletes here. With the scenic mountains, trails, and fresh air, our city is a place that inspires people to pursue healthy and active lives. There are also gyms peppered throughout the community. In fact, Colorado Springs was voted one of the healthiest cities in the United States.[6] A large percentage of the population are workout enthusiasts, including me. I love working out and doing it for fun as well as for my health, but you know I can't do anything half-heartedly. Being competitive by nature, I have competed in men's physique bodybuilding contests for the last several years, so I spend a good bit of time in the gym.

What's interesting is, many mornings at the gym, I find myself watching others work out. For years, I've been watching and learning. I'm a people watcher, an observer who picks up on behavior and nuances. It could be partly because dealing with people in counseling is how God wired me. It's something I've always done at airports, malls, restaurants, the gym, wherever they gather. Human beings are fascinating creatures, and I've picked up a great deal from watching them. At the gym, I've noticed there are typically two types of weight lifters. The first are lifters who stretch before lifting. The second are what I call the *constant contractor* types. They go cold right to the weights and lift hard and heavy, constantly contracting their muscles. This might look great after getting that sought-after pump. However, if all you do is contract them, the body and the muscles specifically react by pulling on each other, causing back pain and all kinds of injuries. I know this because, for years, that was all I knew how to do. After working out, I would leave contracted, and every few months, I would get injured. Years passed where I would repeat this cycle. Finally, fed up with getting injured, I sought out solutions. My search led me to attend several training courses that taught me how to stretch in a way to prevent injury. As a result, stretching a few hours per week became regularly incorporated into my workout routine. This combination has left me injury-free for nearly a decade. The weight lifter who stretches is the second—and better—weight lifter in my opinion.

The same principle applies here as we talk about forgiveness. A warm-up—a mental stretching—needs to be done before doing the Forgiveness for Everyone exercises. It makes the process work smoother and much more effectively. Note that I only have my clients do this exercise before we approach the second part of doing the forgiveness exercises.

"Why?" you might ask. Well, let me give you both my clinical and biblical reasons. Don't skip over this step! If you do, your results will be severely limited in forgiving everyone. This is definitely a key ingredient in the superpower secret sauce that will really enable you to forgive everyone.

Back to the "Why?" Trauma, abuse, and neglect impact your entire being like nothing else in life does. They create a three-dimensional wound. This is not a wound that is three separate wounds—one in your body, one in your soul, one in your spirit. This is one wound encapsulating all that you carry. Some people have several of these three-dimensional wounds. I know because I was one of those people, and out of the five thousand or more clients I have seen in almost forty years of practice, it's safe to say most of them had more than one three-dimensional wound. This warm-up exercise is needed before attempting to forgive each person on your list.

To lacerate such a complex, fully three-dimensional wound, you can't do it one-dimensionally. That is why people who do cognitive therapy alone—aiming to think differently about the trauma, abuse or neglect, or even wrongdoing toward them—get partial healing but still can act or react as if the trauma is not healed. The same applies to those who only do the spiritual work. I've had many well-meaning spiritual leaders or Christian counselor clients do this. Consequently, their symptoms remained because more than their spirit had been impacted. Part of this problem lies in how pastors and counselors are trained. The pastor is strictly trained in Scripture, the counselor trained in the soul, and the medical doctor in the body. However, the Lord has uniquely and graciously cross-trained me. Perhaps it's because of my own three-dimensional wounds of trauma, abuse, and neglect. God taught me through 1 Thessalonians 5:23 that we are spirit, soul, and body. Paul wrote, *"May God Himself, the God of peace, sanctify you through and through. May your whole spirit, soul and body be kept blameless at the coming of our Lord Jesus*

Christ." This clearly shows that we are triune beings. Therefore, we need to lacerate these wounds three-dimensionally and engage all of ourselves in order to fully heal.

But this journey is about our Forgiveness for Everyone, right? Absolutely. However, there is a huge step before forgiveness that makes it significantly easier to do than if you don't take that step. I learned this exercise while working with a teenager in a psychiatric hospital who had been satanically and ritually sexually abused for years. When I was assigned to her, nobody was having any success at a breakthrough. I was still young in my career, and I prayed for revelation. The Holy Spirit prompted me to do something that I felt was insane at the time. With nothing to lose because she wasn't making any progress, I went for it and obeyed what I felt God was telling me to do.

The young girl was able to forgive and started to heal. Amazingly, you could even say, miraculously, her sanity returned. The others working with her were baffled. Shortly afterward, the Lord showed me that what He had told me to do was completely biblical. In fact, Jesus actually laid out the perfect example of doing this. It's one of the few things that is recorded in all four Gospels: Matthew 21:12, Mark 11:15, Luke 19:45, and John 2:14–16. This is the familiar story of Jesus cleansing the temple. It's interesting that He cleansed the temple before He said, "Father, forgive them, for they do not know what they are doing," while hanging on the cross. It's critically important that we do the cleansing-the-temple exercise before going into the Forgiveness for Everyone exercises.

Jesus knew the temple needed to be cleansed because it was being defiled by others who were misusing and abusing it. Paul reminded us in 1 Corinthians 3:16–17 that we are the temple of God. We'll dive into that verse a little deeper in a bit, but if you have been through trauma, abuse, or neglect, then others have misused and abused your temple. These defilements could have been done to you as a child, adolescent, or adult. This affects all of your being: spirit, soul, and body. That's why a simple conversation or even just saying "I forgive you" probably won't discharge the woundedness and rage you could rightfully have. In my book *Intimacy: A 100-Day Guide to Lasting Relationships*, I share this exercise called *cleansing the temple*.[7]

Cleansing the Temple

Cleansing your own temple can remove much of the pain that you may be carrying in your soul. This next point is significant. Even though you did not cause the pain that you experienced, you and I are 100 percent responsible for healing from these wounds. Cleansing the temple has helped many people accelerate their journey to forgive everyone.

Let's start this exercise by examining the places in each Gospel where Jesus cleansed the temple. Take a moment and study each biblical account:

"Jesus entered the temple courts and drove out all who were buying and selling there. He overturned the tables of the money changers and the benches of those selling doves" (Matthew 21:12).

"On reaching Jerusalem, Jesus entered the temple courts and began driving out those who were buying and selling there. He overturned the tables of the money changers and the benches of those selling doves" (Mark 11:15).

"When Jesus entered the temple courts, he began to drive out those who were selling" (Luke 19:45).

"In the temple courts He found people selling cattle, sheep and doves, and others sitting at tables exchanging money. So He made a whip out of cords, and drove all from the temple courts, both sheep and cattle; He scattered the coins of the money changers and overturned their tables. To those who sold doves He said, 'Get these out of here! Stop turning my Father's house into a market!'" (John 2:14–16).

Each of these accounts contains the principles of the temple-cleansing exercise. First, we will review the four major principles, and then we will walk through the practical application of each. The following scripture will be our text for this exercise:

> *When it was almost time for the Jewish Passover, Jesus went up to Jerusalem. In the temple courts He found people selling cattle, sheep and doves, and others sitting at tables exchanging money. So He made a whip out of cords, and drove all from the temple courts, both sheep and cattle; He scattered the coins of the money changers and overturned their tables. To those who sold doves He said, "Get these out of here! Stop turning my Father's house into a market!" His disciples remembered that it is written: "Zeal for your house will consume me."*
>
> *Then the Jews demanded of him, "What miraculous sign can you show us to prove your authority to do all this?"*
>
> *Jesus answered them, "Destroy this temple, and I will raise it again in three days."*
>
> *They replied, "It has taken forty-six years to build this temple, and you are going to raise it in three days?" But the temple He had spoken of was his body. After He was raised from the dead, his disciples recalled what He had said. Then they believed the scripture and the words that Jesus had spoken.* (John 2:13–22)

Biblical Principles

Principle 1: Jesus knew the temple needed to be cleansed.

In most accounts of Jesus cleansing the temple, the temple refers to a physical building in Jerusalem, but in John's account, Jesus refers to His body. John 2:18–21 says, *"The Jews then responded to him, 'What sign can you show us to prove your authority to do all this?' Jesus answered them, 'Destroy this temple, and I will raise it again in three days.' They replied, 'It has taken forty-six years to build this temple, and you are going to raise it in three days?' But the temple he had spoken of was his body."*

This is the first insight into the fact that Jesus was changing the dwelling place of God from the physical temple to the temple of a human being. Paul developed this thought a little later when he recorded that Christian believers are now God's temple. *"Do you not know that you are the temple of God and that the Spirit of God dwells in you? If anyone defiles the temple of God, God will destroy him. For the temple of God is holy, which temple you are"* (1 Corinthians 3:16–17 NKJV).

God's plan all along was to dwell inside of us. We are His holy temple. This being true, our temples can become defiled in a myriad of ways, including manipulation, abuse, and neglect from others. When we get defiled through life, our temple gets defiled as well and needs to be cleaned out.

It's interesting that Jesus, the owner of the temple, was the one who took full responsibility to clean His own temple. He could have made the money changers and sellers of doves who were the perpetrators in the story clean up their own mess, but He didn't. He cleansed the temple. Jesus didn't tell them to cleanse it; He drove them out!

Because you are the possessors of your temple, if it gets defiled through the abuse of others, you are the one who must clean it up. By cleaning His own temple, Jesus sent a clear message to us: We are responsible for cleaning our own temples as well.

Principle 2: Jesus identified the sin that caused the defilement.

In John's rendition of this Gospel event, Jesus stated, *"Get these out of here! Stop turning my Father's house into a market!"* (2:16). In Luke 19:46, Jesus' words are slightly stronger: *"It is written,"* He said to them, *"'My house will be a house of prayer'; but you have made it 'a den of robbers.'"* Mark 11:17 and Matthew 21:13 are very similar. Jesus made it crystal clear to the people why He was cleansing the temple. They were taking something holy and misusing it to profit themselves. Most of the people who have hurt you have no concept of your holiness or preciousness, and you must call out the sin or damage that has been done to you by those who have defiled your temple.

Principle 3: Jesus engaged His anger at the injustice.

Jesus was able to engage His anger at the injustice both verbally and physically. No doubt, turning over the tables created quite a scene. On top of that, Jesus was a carpenter before power tools existed, and walking was His primary mode of transportation. He was in shape and probably had a seriously low body-fat-to-muscle ratio. In other words, Jesus was much a man and if He became angry, you wouldn't want to be in His way. Of course, the Jews challenged His authority to create such a ruckus. The enemy never likes it when we take authority and cleanse our temple.

How do I know this was a premeditated act on Jesus' part? Look further at John's account of the cleansing of the temple. *"In the temple courts He found people selling cattle, sheep and doves, and others sitting at tables exchanging money. So He made a whip out of cords"* (John 2:14–15). This passage gives us the sense that Jesus was looking around and witnessing the people's mistreatment of His holy temple. Then, in verse 15, He gets a bundle of cords and takes the time to make a whip. Now, I don't know how long it took Jesus to make a whip—maybe minutes, maybe hours—but He had already decided to use that whip when He entered His temple to cleanse it. With every weave of the cords, Jesus knew what He was about to do.

As we proceed with this exercise, you will need to make choices to prioritize your time to prepare for cleansing your temple. Those who go about this intentionally and purposefully have received great breakthroughs in their lives.

Principle 4: The temple was restored to its original order.

The story of Jesus cleansing the temple offers a picture of how to heal the wounds inside your temple. After Jesus engaged His righteous rage and sent the defilers out, His temple was cleansed. Only Jesus had the power to cleanse His own temple. No other prophet or king had done so before Him or after Him. He alone could clean His house. In the same way, we alone can clean our own temples.

Jesus wasn't merely having a bad day. This was a specific and intentional, sovereign act of His will. It was a well-thought-out act of obedience. It's important to understand this point because it will take an intentional act of your will to clean your temple. You have to resolve in your heart and mind to act. Fear will try to paralyze you, but action cures fear. Once you walk through the rest of the exercises, I believe it will become an act of obedience to God as well.

I have been fortunate to help people in both inpatient psychiatric hospitals and outpatient office settings. Many of these souls had experienced trauma in one form or another, and their wounds were lodged deep in the core of their beings. Like them, people may have hurt you at the core of your being. You may have presumed that you've forgiven them. Nevertheless, the bullet is still inside, and the wound is festering. The muck and defilement are still surrounding it. That doesn't necessarily mean you didn't forgive them; it just means that you haven't cleansed your temple yet.

The concept I'm about to suggest to you may seem foreign or uncomfortable at first.

My experience with cleansing the temple has been nothing short of miraculous. Sexual-abuse survivors tend to heal unusually quickly after this exercise. Women who have been sexually betrayed by their husbands seem to move through the stages of grief and forgiveness at an accelerated pace compared to those who refuse to cleanse their temple.

No matter how you have experienced woundedness or betrayal, keep an open mind and try this exercise. Only after you've gone through it will you know whether it's been effective or not. I tell my clients they can have an opinion after they do the exercise, but they need to just trust the process and see the results for themselves.

This exercise is to be done separately for each person who has hurt you. Please don't combine people. Each wound is unique and deserves individual attention in order to fully heal. Keeping each person separate may seem like more work, but it is imperative to optimize your ability to give forgiveness to everyone.

To prepare for the exercise, get a pad of paper or use your phone notes, but make sure it's somewhere private. Then, make a list of the people who have hurt you. This list doesn't have to be in any particular order, and many clients add to it once they start experiencing the freedom. My suggestion is to start with the lesser of the offenses and move toward the worst, but some people prefer to hit the big ones first.

Now, you are ready to begin the exercise.

The "Cleansing the Temple" Exercise

1. Write an anger letter.

The first step in cleansing your temple is to write an anger letter to the person who has hurt you, a letter you will not send. Imagine this person in the room with you, but he or she is unable to talk or move. You can say whatever you need to say to him or her in this letter. This is not a time to suppress your feelings but rather to vent all the thoughts and feelings of hate, disgust, and anguish that have been robbing your soul. Neither is this an "I forgive you" letter. That will come later. This is the place where you rid yourself of the anger that has been a part of your soul.

Here are some guidelines for writing an effective letter: Do not watch your language or grammar. Simply spill your emotions onto the page or screen. Bleed all over the pages. Don't hold back. Write as long a letter as you need. It may be one page or many pages. You will know intuitively when you are finished. Lastly, never send the letter or read it to that person, especially if it's to your spouse. The purpose of the letter is for *your* healing, and nobody needs to read it but you. My recommendation is when you are done with the entire cleaning of your temple, per person, rip the letters into pieces, throw them away, or maybe burn them.

2. Read your letter aloud.

Once you have written your letter, read it out loud. Some people have strong feelings that come out when they do this. If this happens, know that it is normal. However, just because you've vented strong feelings doesn't mean you are finished. Other people may be numb and have a difficult time expressing their feelings. That is normal too. If your offender's name is Toby, then your letter might start as follows: "Toby, how could you have done this to me? I trusted you!" Of course, Toby is nowhere around. You certainly don't need to do this where anyone can overhear you. You need to be in a room alone reading the letter aloud. The reason this step in the exercise is so critical is that your brain needs to know where you are going as you continue in the process of cleansing your temple.

3. Get warmed up.

In Jesus' situation, He made a whip. I don't recommend whips, but a padded baseball bat or metal tennis racket that won't break could be helpful. After that, begin warming up your body. Take your bat and hit a mattress or pillow with small hits. Strike the bed using medium, large, and extra-large hits. Do this three times. Warm up your voice as well. Shout "No!" each time you hit the bed or pillow. Use soft, normal, loud, and shouting levels with your voice. This may feel awkward, but releasing the buildup of pain from your soul and spirit is like puking after a bad meal. That is why it's important to be warmed up physically. While you're warming up, make sure you are home alone and disconnect the phone so that you are not disturbed. Note: Before doing this, if you have a heart condition or other medical condition that warrants talking to your medical doctor first, please do so.

4. Engage your anger physically and verbally.

After reading your letter and warming up, pick up your bat. Hit the bed or pillow and symbolically let "Toby" have it. You can yell, scream, and cry, whatever it takes to release the infection that has been harming you. You can symbolically tell "Toby" that his secrets are not controlling you anymore. He was to blame! You have no limits as to what you can say to your offender. For once, let go of all the emotional control that is keeping this wound infected. Let it out!

Carrying pain inside causes you to protect yourself from being hurt. I've seen symptoms of trauma, abuse, or neglect disappear shortly after doing this exercise. Please don't rob yourself of healing by thinking that this is silly or irrational. In my forty years of experience, it's been amazing to observe, time and again, that those who resist doing this the most actually get the most out of it when they finally do it. Sadly, those who believe the exercise is beneath them and don't do it usually stay stuck.

The hitting, screaming, and letting the pus out of this three-dimensional wound can last from fifteen minutes to an hour. Like when writing the letter, you will know when to stop; your body will let you know when you have spiritually, emotionally, and physically put this behind you.

Someone has given you toxic poison, and you have been carrying it in your body, soul, and spirit ever since. After you remove it, you'll feel like a brand-new person. Don't you think you are worth getting all that junk out? I think you are. So does the One who loves you most.

Before we move on, I want to stress the importance of working on one offender at a time. If three different people have offended you, then you will need to complete three different sessions. Do not try to go through this exercise just once for all the people who have offended you. Each "bullet" needs to be extracted separately.

It's common to have different experiences and gain helpful insight while working through your list. I've known men and women who thought offender number one was the worst. Yet, an offender whom they considered less significant produced a more explosive, more intense venting experience for them.

Intentionally set some time aside when you can have the house to yourself to get this very important work done. If you have children, ask your spouse to take them somewhere for a couple of hours. The time you invest in getting this pus out of your system can help you be a better spouse and parent.

I'm not going to exaggerate or sugarcoat it. Doing this is hard, messy work. But countless souls have been set free by doing this and the other exercises in the following pages. If you could scroll through my memory bank and see the thousands of changed lives and happy endings I've witnessed from people doing this work, you would get on it right away!

Finally, some people have found it helpful to be accountable to someone during the process. Their accountability partner doesn't have to know the story or the people on your list. You can just say you are reading a book, and you need to do some exercises and want to be accountable to do them by such and such a date. This could help you stay focused on the task. Some people do weekends in a hotel to work through the list. Whatever it takes, do it. Jesus and your family are all worthy of you releasing these wounds and being healed in the process. Can you imagine all the sludge and junk people have placed in your temple washed out of you with a power washer? You now have that clean Irish scent inside your soul. You are lighter in so many ways, enabling you to keep traveling this path of forgiveness.

CHAPTER SEVEN

Commanded

Climbing this sometimes rugged and jagged mountain on our journey of forgiveness is undoubtedly a challenging endeavor. It's definitely not for the faint of heart, as it requires faith, courage, determination, and grace—*lots* of grace. Truth be told, this journey is bigger than our ability to pull it off alone. Allowing the Lord to empower us and, at times, carry us up the steepest and rockiest slopes is the only way we can hope to reach the peak.

The good news, according to Paul in 2 Corinthians 12:9–10, is that God's grace IS sufficient, and His power is made perfect in our weakness, and that when we are weak, He is strong. The Lord will empower us along the way. Even when the atmosphere gets thin, the oxygen is low, and we feel we can't possibly take another step. It's then that we must take our rest, then choose to continue climbing the mountain with Him, trusting Him. That's where faith and courage come in. But for those who make it to the mountaintop, the reward is life-altering. When on the summit, everything changes because you now are viewing things from an elevated perspective. You can see for miles and miles. Not only does the landscape below look different, but people do, too, including those who hurt you. Instead of looking at them from the lower elevations where you sometimes can't see through them, or around them, or what they did to you, now you are viewing them from a higher plane. You are not better than them, but you're above the actions that wounded you. You are seeing beyond. Instead of a narrow focus on that person or those people, they become mere dots against the broad horizon and endless vistas of freedom.

Not everyone, however, makes it to the top. Many find the climb too rigorous and simply give up. Some never start. Choosing forgiveness, especially for everyone, seems too lofty and unattainable. Instead of trusting God to empower them, they allow the fear of never being free to replace faith. Living with pain and unforgiveness has become comfortable. In John 5:6, Jesus asked the paralytic, "Do you want to be healed?" Interesting question. You would think it'd be a no-brainer. But not everybody does. Others don't believe they can be.

As you travel on your journey to the summit, you might be asking why everyone doesn't take this journey, or why some start but quit when the trail gets steep. I have asked myself the same questions. However, I have learned to be content that the Lord calls those He calls, and some follow and some delay, while others make excuses and never take the adventure they are called to. They choose to stay stuck.

Ascending this mountain of Forgiveness for Everyone reminds me of a character in the Bible who made a trek up a significant mountain. What's interesting is he was not meant to go all alone, yet he did. Exodus 19 tells a fascinating story about Moses talking to God. God told Moses He wanted all the people of Israel to come close enough to hear Him talk to Moses. The Lord told Moses to have the people consecrate themselves and not go up the mountain until they were called. Now imagine this invitation to draw closer to the Father: *"The LORD would speak to Moses face to face, as one speaks to a friend"* (Exodus 33:11). Wow. God spoke to him as to a friend. Moses was as close to God as any man in the flesh could get at that time, and out of their conversation, Moses wrote what has become the foundation of the Western world. The justice systems, medical insights, governmental obligations, human rights, and almost all of our laws have their roots in the writings of Moses. Could you imagine how different the world would have been if the entire nation of Israel had gotten close enough to God to hear Him like Moses did, or like Adam and Eve heard Him walking in the garden? Each person would have had a God encounter. The fear of the Lord, which leads to all wisdom, could have been released on an entire nation.

Let's read the story.

> *The LORD said to Moses, "I am going to come to you in a dense cloud, so that the people will hear me speaking with you and will always put their trust in you." Then Moses told the LORD what the people had said.*
>
> *And the LORD said to Moses, "Go to the people and consecrate them today and tomorrow. Have them wash their clothes and be ready by the third day, because on that day, the LORD will come down on Mount Sinai in the sight of all the people. Put limits for the people around the mountain and tell them, 'Be careful that you do not approach the mountain or touch the foot of it. Whoever touches the mountain is to be put to death . . .'"*

After Moses had gone down the mountain to the people, he consecrated them, and they washed their clothes. Then he said to the people, "Prepare yourselves for the third day. Abstain from sexual relations."

*On the morning of the third day there was thunder and lightning, with a thick cloud over the mountain, and a very loud trumpet blast. Everyone in the camp trembled. Then Moses led the people out of the camp to meet with God, and they stood at the foot of the mountain. Mount Sinai was covered with smoke, because the L*ORD *descended on it in fire. The smoke billowed up from it like smoke from a furnace, and the whole mountain trembled violently. As the sound of the trumpet grew louder and louder, Moses spoke, and the voice of God answered him.*

*The L*ORD *descended to the top of Mount Sinai and called Moses to the top of the mountain. So Moses went up and the L*ORD *said to him, "Go down and warn the people so they do not force their way through to see the L*ORD *and many of them perish. Even the priests, who approach the L*ORD*, must consecrate themselves, or the L*ORD *will break out against them."*

*Moses said to the L*ORD*, "The people cannot come up Mount Sinai, because you yourself warned us, 'Put limits around the mountain and set it apart as holy.'"*

> *The LORD replied, "Go down and bring Aaron up with you. But the priests and the people must not force their way through to come up to the LORD, or he will break out against them."*
>
> *So Moses went down to the people and told them.* (Exodus 19:9–25)

Then, in Exodus 20, God spoke the Ten Commandments to Moses, and the people responded in the following manner:

> *When the people saw the thunder and lightning and heard the trumpet and saw the mountain in smoke, they trembled with fear. They stayed at a distance and said to Moses, "Speak to us yourself and we will listen. But do not have God speak to us or we will die."*
>
> *Moses said to the people, "Do not be afraid. God has come to test you, so that the fear of God will be with you to keep you from sinning."*
>
> *The people remained at a distance, while Moses approached the thick darkness where God was.* (Exodus 20:18–21)

This is one of the greatest yet most neglected stories in Scripture. Here's a man of God, Moses, who the Israelites knew had been meeting with God. Now, God was giving the whole nation a day when they could meet with Him. But instead of delighting in the Divine invitation, they shrunk back out of fear and said, "No, we won't go up to Him." So, Moses went up the mountain alone and received the Ten Commandments. When he came back down, he gave the people the laws of God. We know their history. At times, the Hebrews followed God's laws, and at times, they chose to disobey. As a result, they were disciplined by the Lord. These laws and the ideas in them were meant to protect them and be a lifestyle of blessing for themselves and their families. *"If you fully obey the* Lord *your God and carefully follow all His commands I give you today, the* Lord *your God will set you high above all the nations on earth. All these blessings will come on you and accompany you if you obey the* Lord *your God"* (Deuteronomy 28:1–2).

There is another person in Scripture who came from the mountain of God called heaven. He, too, came to share with us the heart of God for us to be blessed when we follow His ideas and commandments. John writes it this way: *"In the beginning was the Word, and the Word was with God, and the Word was God. He was with God in the beginning."* Then, Christ, who is the Word in heaven, came to earth. *"The Word became flesh and made His dwelling among us. We have seen His glory, the glory of the one and only Son, who came from the Father, full of grace and truth."* (John 1:1–2, 14).

Believing that Christ came from heaven to earth is foundational to the Christian faith. Like Moses, He, too, wanted to share the heart of the Father. One of the most memorable interactions Jesus had with the religious leaders was when they asked Him which is the greatest commandment:

> *And one of the scribes came, and having heard them reasoning together, and perceiving that he had answered them well, asked him, Which is the first commandment of all?*
>
> *And Jesus answered him, The first of all the commandments is, Hear, O Israel; The Lord our God is one Lord:*
>
> *And thou shalt love the Lord thy God with all thy heart, and with all thy soul, with all thy mind, and with all thy strength: this is the first commandment.*
>
> *And the second is like, namely this, Thou shalt love thy neighbour as thyself. There is none other commandment greater than these.* (Mark 12:28–31 KJV)

This whole idea of commandments, especially to Western believers, is quite a challenge. Jesus was talking from a kingdom perspective in which we are in a kingdom but are not the king. That has been a major struggle of mankind ever since Adam. Adam was commanded not to eat the fruit from the Tree of the

Knowledge of Good and Evil. This clear and simple command was to let Adam know he was not king in the garden, but rather the Father was King.

In Jesus' day, monarchy was the primary form of government. Everyone understood that there were kings, and most people were subjects of those kings. You did as you were told, regardless of your thoughts, opinions, or feelings. The law was the law, and you followed it. Living in a democratic republic with many freedoms, we feel we have a right to everything from voting to parking spots to being heard and having our feelings validated. If we don't agree, we might not keep that law or commandment of our government.

While our freedom is a beautiful thing, and our freedoms were fought and died for, I think living in a democratic republic makes it more difficult to grasp what it means to be a true Kingdom follower. John the Baptist and Jesus both preached the Kingdom of God, but it wasn't an "if it feels good, do it" kingdom where, if you don't agree, you can decide what you will or will not do. In a true kingdom it's, "Yes, sir. What's the question, sir?" In a democracy it's, "I'll get back to you and let you know if I agree or not."

Democracy and a republic are wonderful forms of government to protect citizens from evil men and evil schemes to limit citizens' free will. God is all about free will. However, though God gives us free will, the Kingdom of God doesn't work as a democracy. That's because, unlike fallen man, God is perfect. He IS love. There is no evil in Him. He is perfectly just, perfectly holy, perfectly good. There is no inconsistency in Him. He is the Creator of the universe. He is God. He has the right to give and take life and be just. The more we mature in Christ, the more we find ourselves detaching from the culture and its ways. Not disengaging, but detaching. There's a difference. We have to forsake our culture and integrate the truth that we, as believers, are in a kingdom that is not of this world with an all-powerful, all-knowing King who gives us the breath of life. We are to reverently respect Him, fear Him, and know that He loves us deeply enough to die for us. Any of His commands are here to be a blessing for us.

Now, I'm sure some of you are thinking, *Dr. Weiss, what does all of this have to do with Forgiveness for Everyone?* A lot. And here's why: In this part of the journey, some people clearly see the heart and will of the Father. However, instead of embracing His goodness for making a way to be reconciled with Him through what Christ did on the cross, they shrink back and disobey. The problem is, the King—the Father, Son, and Holy Spirit in One—is not suggesting but commanding, and

He's just in doing so. Read the following verses carefully. They explain it well.

> *Jesus answered, "Most assuredly, I say to you, unless one is born of water and the Spirit, he cannot enter the kingdom of God. That which is born of the flesh is flesh, and that which is born of the Spirit is spirit.*
>
> *. . . For God so loved the world that He gave His only begotten Son, that whoever believes in Him should not perish but have everlasting life.*
>
> *. . . He who believes in Him is not condemned; but he who does not believe is condemned already, because he has not believed in the name of the only begotten Son of God."* (John 3:5–6, 16, 18 NKJV)

That's pretty clear-cut. Receiving God's provision through Jesus and entering His Kingdom is not a suggestion. It's a command. If you don't believe and receive, you are condemned. That idea causes bristles to rise like porcupines to our entitled, democratic-style society. Still, it is God's way. Unbelief is a sin. In essence, unbelief is rejecting God's Kingship. Once we repent, receive His gift of provision, and enter the Kingdom, we now live under the rules of the King with other commands. Yet, He's a loving and graceful Ruler whom we can trust. His rules are to bring us life and life more abundantly.

It's when we don't trust and try to go it our own way that we mess up. Thankfully, if we are His, He is there to pick us up and set us back on the path.

Next, I want to go through some of these commands, particularly of Jesus, to help us stay motivated for the next chapter, where we actually do the forgiving exercises. Before we get into this part of the woods, though, I want to state clearly, as a psychologist and fellow traveler, that I respect and honor the journey some of you are on. I understand that with your level of pain and trauma, it can take time to arrive at forgiveness—longer for some than for others. That's okay. Take as much time as you need. However, I think it will become evident that Jesus does not give us much fudge room when it comes to the journey itself, which is required by the Father.

Let's start with the ever-so-famous Lord's Prayer. Jesus taught His disciples how to pray in Matthew 6:9–13 KJV:

> *After this manner therefore pray ye: Our Father which art in heaven, Hallowed be thy name.*
>
> *Thy kingdom come, Thy will be done in earth, as it is in heaven.*
>
> *Give us this day our daily bread.*
>
> *And forgive us our debts, as we forgive our debtors.*

And lead us not into temptation, but deliver us from evil: For thine is the kingdom, and the power, and the glory, for ever. Amen.

One of the fascinating parts of this prayer is that Jesus teaches us to ask for forgiveness of our debts as we forgive our debtors. Right there, it would have been clear in Jesus' mind that there was some connection or interdependence between us being forgiving of others and us being forgiven ourselves by the Father. Immediately after sharing His prayer, Jesus highlighted the same point again of how important this forgiveness thing is to the Father: *For if ye forgive men their trespasses, your heavenly Father will also forgive you: But if ye forgive not men their trespasses, neither will your Father forgive your trespasses"* (Matthew 6:14–15 KJV).

Jesus' statement here is shockingly blunt and unmistakable: Forgive and be forgiven. Don't forgive, don't be forgiven. Jesus' words give us a glimpse into how He thinks about the importance of us living in a forgiveness state of being. Kingdom life turns on the hinge of forgiveness.

Peter, who was trying to wrap his mind around this whole forgiveness thing, asked Jesus about forgiving the guy who continued to abuse him. Read Jesus' parabolic response:

Then came Peter to him, and said, Lord, how oft shall my brother sin against me, and I forgive him? till seven times?

Jesus saith unto him, I say not unto thee, Until seven times: but, Until seventy times seven.

Therefore is the kingdom of heaven likened unto a certain king, which would take account of his servants.

And when he had begun to reckon, one was brought unto him, which owed him ten thousand talents.

But forasmuch as he had not to pay, his lord commanded him to be sold, and his wife, and children, and all that he had, and payment to be made.

The servant therefore fell down, and worshipped him, saying, Lord, have patience with me, and I will pay thee all.

Then the lord of that servant was moved with compassion, and loosed him, and forgave him the debt.

But the same servant went out, and found one of his fellowservants, which owed him an hundred pence: and he laid hands on him, and took him by the throat, saying, Pay me that thou owest.

And his fellowservant fell down at his feet, and besought him, saying, Have patience with me, and I will pay thee all.

And he would not: but went and cast him into prison, till he should pay the debt.

> *So when his fellowservants saw what was done, they were very sorry, and came and told unto their lord all that was done.*
>
> *Then his lord, after that he had called him, said unto him, O thou wicked servant, I forgave thee all that debt, because thou desiredst me:*
>
> *Shouldest not thou also have had compassion on thy fellowservant, even as I had pity on thee?*
>
> *And his lord was wroth, and delivered him to the tormentors, till he should pay all was due unto him.*
>
> *So likewise shall my heavenly Father do also unto you, if ye from your hearts forgive not every one his brother their trespasses.* (Matthew 18:21–35 KJV)

There is so much here that could be discussed. I just want to highlight a couple of critical points. First, it's not the amount of sin that's the issue; it's our heart's disposition toward that sin. For God, the issue is whether we are gracious and humble or demanding of retribution. Do we recognize our own fallenness and need for grace? Or are we like the proud, self-righteous Pharisee? I know that may seem shallow, especially when our bitterness and unforgiveness stem from heartbreaking sins against us, like a drunk driver running over our child, being sexually abused, or being betrayed by a spouse whom you gave your life to and trusted. Again, for those deeper sins, the journey to forgiveness can be rigorous and long. It takes the Lord to carry us and make us strong in our weakness. That said, as believers, we must hear the Father's heart regarding forgiveness.

Second, there are only two times Jesus refers to a wicked servant. Here, when it relates to not forgiving, and in Matthew 25 with the parable of the lazy servant. I never want to be seen by my Master as wicked either way, as being unwilling to take the journey of forgiveness or by being lazy toward His calling in my life.

In Luke 6:35–37, Jesus gave similar insights into how the Father thinks about forgiveness. Again, these are not suggestions. They are rules for Kingdom life.

> *But love ye your enemies, and do good, and lend, hoping for nothing again; and your reward shall be great, and ye shall be the children of the Highest: for He is kind unto the unthankful and to the evil.*
>
> *Be ye therefore merciful, as your Father also is merciful.*
>
> *Judge not, and ye shall not be judged: condemn not, and ye shall not be condemned: forgive, and ye shall be forgiven . . .* (KJV).

Here's another one:

Then said He unto the disciples, It is impossible but that offences will come: but woe unto him, through whom they come!

It were better for him that a millstone were hanged about his neck, and he cast into the sea, than that he should offend one of these little ones.

Take heed to yourselves: If thy brother trespass against thee, rebuke him; and if he repent, forgive him.

And if he trespass against thee seven times in a day, and seven times in a day turn again to thee, saying, I repent; thou shalt forgive him.

And the apostles said unto the Lord, Increase our faith.

And the Lord said, If ye had faith as a grain of mustard seed, ye might say unto this sycamine tree, Be thou plucked up by the root, and be thou planted in the sea; and it should obey you. (Luke 17:1–6 KJV)

This scripture is rich with insight. I love the way Jesus starts this teaching with an assumption that offenses will come. Jesus normalizes that people hurt people and that in life, it's impossible to escape being sinned against. In his renowned Bible commentary, Matthew Henry wrote concerning Luke 17:1,

"Faith in God's pardoning mercy will enable us to get over the greatest difficulties in the way of forgiving our brethren. As with God, nothing is impossible, so all things are possible to him that can believe. Our Lord showed His disciples their need of deep humility."[8]

Then Jesus addressed the person who keeps repenting and asking for forgiveness over and over. The apostle's response was epic. "Increase our faith," Jesus answered them in verse 6, with a quick edification on mustard seed faith. This is a well-used scripture that is often taken out of context, but it's about having faith like a mustard seed in the context of moving the mountains that others put in our path by their sin toward us. It takes real faith, and by that I mean heroic faith, to do the hard work of forgiving people who have hurt our spirit, soul, and body. Real faith, facing real pain in real relationships, is what this scripture is referring to. Yet, if we bring our little mustard seed of faith to forgive those who trespass against us, we can see that mountain move right out of our hearts and be cast into the sea, and our hearts will never see that mountain again. I don't know about you, but I would rather cast a mountain into the sea than climb it any day!

For a moment, imagine the worst wound that is causing you pain yanked out of your heart, thrown out and drowned in a big sea of forgetfulness, never to come up again. I have experienced this, and so have thousands of others as they forgive everyone. It truly is like a sea of forgetfulness. The facts are still available to us, but the festering and oozing pain is no longer with us. It's amazing, and I would encourage you to follow the Father's heart on this forgiveness idea and command. Christ Jesus came from the mountain in heaven not only to forgive us our sins but to empower us as His children to not allow the sins or offenses of others to slow us down in life.

The apostle Paul touched on this in a gentle manner: *"And be ye kind one to another, tenderhearted, forgiving one another, even as God for Christ's sake hath forgiven you"* (Ephesians 4:32 KJV). In our hearts, we know we are commanded to forgive, not just once, but seventy times seven. It's bigger than us, but as we agree with God and take the leap of faith, He will infuse us with His superpower of grace that is sufficient and turn our weakness into strength. But why are we commanded to love, give, and forgive? I believe it's for our own sake. God wants us to worship Him so we are grounded every day in the reality of who He is. And as we focus on a loving

God, we can become loving as well. When we love each other, we are more like Him. He is perfect and would have had the right to destroy us all. Instead, He went to the cross and died for us.

When we forgive, love, and give, we are becoming more like Him, and more of Him is flowing out of us toward others. Understand that you don't need to go to your perpetrators to do all this. Just as Jesus could stand in one place and command a demon to leave or heal someone from miles away, so we can forgive at a distance. The Father still sees our hearts becoming more like His as we are able to forgive everyone.

Forgiving is for our good. It allows us not to be controlled by the past or the people in the past. The peak of the mountain gives us an elevated perspective and freedom to grow in an unlimited manner as His love flows through us. When we forgive the other person, we unhook from them and can drive our car without any pull from their wrongdoing. All of God's commandments are for our benefit. Our very essence—spirit, soul, and body—isn't designed to harbor resentment. When we obey God's Word and do the work necessary to get us there, we are truly setting ourselves up for a better life.

I know this personally. I never met my father, had experienced abandonment, and had been sexually abused by both men and women—and when I did my work of giving forgiveness to everyone, I became free of the people and situations of the past. And I didn't get all knotted up or weird when those conversations came up. God used my experience to give me the medicine to help others heal and the ability to pass that medicine on to you.

You have the opportunity ahead of you in the next chapter to do some challenging work so you, too, can look more like Jesus. You can also experience your faith being matured and know what it feels like to see mountains evaporate right before you. I have seen thousands cast their mountains into the sea and walk much freer from the heart. You deserve this freedom, and you are on this journey. So, as any guide worth his salt would say, "Keep walking. The view is just a ways away!"

CHAPTER EIGHT

Everybody Has a Story

The sun is setting, dropping a velvet blanket of pink and purple behind the distant peaks. There's nothing quite like sunset in the mountains. It's also the Creator's way of letting us know it will soon be dark and is time to set up camp.

As your guide, I would ensure we stop early enough to get our tents out of our bags and pitched. Continuing to hike through the rocky and winding forest at night would be extremely dangerous and unwise, not to mention scary. Dusk beckons hikers to settle in but is a wake-up call for nocturnal creatures to crawl out from their cracks, caves, and gullies. Of course, not all of them are predators looking to inflict harm.

A simple squirrel or a couple of chipmunks scurrying around in the darkness, however, can sound a lot like a prowling mountain lion or snoopy bear! Don't worry. We'll scatter a few lanterns around the camp and build a nice fire. After filling our canteens with crystal-clear snowmelt spring water and tossing a few steaks with roasted corn on the grill, we'll be ready to chow down while enjoying some more laid-back conversation. This is no ordinary hike, so we are staying on task for our journey to forgive everyone.

Leading off the dialogue, I encourage those gathered to open up by sharing their own stories, yet without going into too much detail. Because the atmosphere feels so safe, though, some do go into detail, like Charles, a thirty-five-year-old government employee. Super responsible, he has a wife and two small children. His story doesn't start off like you would expect. "Based on some of what I picked up of your stories on the trail," Charles begins, "I'm sure I am not like most of you."

He pauses a moment, considering his words, then sets down his thermos before continuing. "What I am going to start off with might not make sense to you at all. I had perfect parents. I really mean it. They were authentic in their love for God and for me. I always felt loved and heard in my family. I got disciplined, but only when I really needed it. My younger brother and sister were great. No real conflict between us. She's a missionary, and my brother just finished medical school.

"My parents never cursed or argued in front of us kids. We always had enough and were comfortable. And yes, my dad actually went to every function and game he could. The two of us still go out in the backyard sometimes and toss a ball around. It sounds like the perfect childhood, and it would have been except for the villain in my story. That would be me. I was the problem. In high school, I started messing with drugs—just pot to start with. My parents didn't have a clue. I still went to church and even taught Sunday school. Bit by bit, the drugs got worse, and then alcohol started to get a grip on me. It was pretty much when I was out partying with friends. I knew when I needed to be sober enough before going home. If my parents had a flaw, it was that they trusted me maybe a little too much.

"I was having sex when I could and even got drunk one night, which led to an encounter with a college guy. It freaked me out, and I started spiraling. But because I was heading to college that fall, I somehow held it together. In college, I figured out that if I stayed sober for a few days, I could get my schoolwork done, and nobody, including my professors, would be the wiser. Women were attracted to me, so they weren't hard to get. Even so, I started frequenting strip clubs and adult bookstores.

"Not long out of college, I met the woman of my dreams. She was the one, and I straightened up for a while. Purehearted and faithful, we agreed to do it God's way and wait until we married. After marriage, however, I continued to struggle secretly with sexual issues. Then, my closet self was exposed when I got caught lurking in the shadows of a strip club. The news hit my precious wife like a sledgehammer. She felt betrayed, humiliated, and wept so hard I thought she was going to die. During that confrontation, a couple of other secrets of mine got spilled, and just like that, I was out of my own house for a couple of months while we tried to figure things out. Through everything, my wife was amazing. I can't believe she continues to love me like she does. She eventually forgave me and trusted me again, but I'm a mess. I can't forgive myself. I don't even like me."

Charles pauses, figuring he's said too much, but the faces looking back at him are filled with compassion and empathy. "Well, I guess that's about it," he says with a nod.

No sooner has Charles taken a sip from his thermos than Heidi jumps in. "That's funny, Charles," she says. "I think together our stories would make a complete mess." There are a few chuckles because some there already know Heidi's story.

"Actually," she continues, "I'm just the opposite of Charles. My start was pretty bad, like really bad. I never met my biological mother or father. The nuns tell me I was dropped off one morning at their monastery with no information. I don't remember anything about the nuns because I wasn't there too long. At three years old, a couple adopted me. They already had two boys who were a good bit older than me. They were now my mom, dad, and brothers. Then, sometime before the first grade, my dad started sexually abusing me. It was so bad, I hated hearing him walk up the stairs to my room, and enter through a door I couldn't lock myself. Around third grade, my brother started to do the same thing. He must have told my other brother, and he started to abuse me sexually too. This went on somewhat regularly, and it's a miracle I didn't get pregnant.

"When I was twelve and told my mom, she beat me so hard, calling me a liar and slut to even think of such a thing. I don't want to believe she knew, but how could she not? From that day forward, I had no family, just abusers. As a teen, alcohol, older boys, and men fit the same bill. They looked normal but used me, and I started to use them. I was spiraling out of control, like

Charles. Instead of going to college, though, I became a flight attendant and would pick up guys in first class.

"Well, as you can guess," Heidi goes on, "I got pregnant and had no idea who my baby's father was. I had a beautiful daughter and married a guy when she was one. Later, I found out he was frequenting prostitutes and into all kinds of weird sex stuff. He gave me an STD while I was pregnant with my second child. I stayed for the children but got divorced when they were in grade school. I went back on the prowl hunting men and found a decent, God-fearing man. We dated for two years and married. He is the real deal and loves me and my children like they are his own.

"We're still married, but I can feel myself being what my therapist calls *dysfunctional*, especially if I feel rejected or stressed. I also have a problem keeping a job because of my explosive anger. Sometimes, I just explode because there is so much built up inside me. I've got a load of people to work through forgiving. I never thought about forgiving myself, but I think I'm going to add myself to the list."

Nina jumps in and says, "I'm so sorry that all happened, Heidi. I can't imagine that. My story is so opposite. I knew who my mom was, but I never really knew her. You know? She always had dinner on the table and helped with homework, but we never had a heart-to-heart, mother-daughter type of relationship, and she is almost seventy. I never heard her praise me or my siblings or even my dad. I never saw her kiss my dad, and she always pushed him away like she was embarrassed by him. Dad stayed away a lot. He always seemed to be traveling for business or something.

"When I was twelve, my world fell apart as my mom was on the phone with my dad, and all I heard her say was, 'What do you mean, you're not coming home?' My dad was the principal of my junior high school, and he moved in with the gym teacher at school. It was the weirdest thing, and after that, my mom couldn't get it together. She went through severe depression, which affected all of us. Surprisingly, though, a year or so later, Dad came back home, and things between them seemed better. Yet, neither of them were really connected to us kids. It was like we were functioning together but not relating at all.

"In college," Nina continues, "I was shy with boys and really didn't want to date. I did have a few encounters, but I never felt like I gave my heart to anyone. Even in marriage, I feel more like my mom than I would like to admit. My husband is kind, but I can tell he feels unloved, and I feel fearful to jump all in. So yeah, I have to forgive some stuff, but I don't know how to do that."

Everyone is nodding as person after person shares their story of neglect, trauma, abuse, and wrongdoings. Why don't you join us? Go ahead and picture yourself sitting around the fire in this scene, opening up your heart. It's not that hard. If you felt free and unjudged, what would you say?

Think about that, and even if you are by yourself and need to look over your anger list to jog your memory, go ahead. Have that conversation. Go sit on your porch, in your favorite chair, and tell your story. It can be helpful to at least feel like you shared it. And if you have never shared it with another person, you would benefit tremendously from doing so.

A Divine Encounter

I'll never forget sitting in a psychiatric hospital as a mental health technician for alcohol and drug addicts. This was a great job during my seminary years. I mostly worked the 3–11 p.m. shift and would go with the patients to their classes on addiction and recovery, as well as to their various twelve-step groups. Once, during a twelve-step class, I was reading through the steps and realized the Lord had taken me through most of them. I alluded to this earlier when I went to everyone and asked for forgiveness. However, there were two steps that haunted me. The more I understood recovery as I was becoming an alcohol and drug addiction counselor, the more I knew I personally needed to do these two steps. The two steps I am referring to are steps 4 and 5. Many alcoholics or addicts of any kind tend to pull back and skip over these two steps.

Step 4 reads: "Made a searching and fearless moral inventory of ourselves." Step 5 reads: "Admitted to God ourselves and to another human being the exact nature of our wrongs." Even though I was professionally helping many people at the time, the Holy Spirit was prompting me to do this in my own life. I'm not going to lie. It was a tough act of obedience to trust God and another person with the big, bad secrets I still had. What if the person I chose rejected me or, worse, told other people? I would be humiliated and devastated. Regardless, I knew the Holy Spirit was leading, and it was time to do these two steps.

So, I dove into my life story and made a list of all of it—the good, the bad, and the ugly. I had some *good*. After all, the Lord had saved, healed, and delivered me, and so much good was in my life at this point.

I definitely had some *bad*. This was the stuff that I wasn't proud of and had never told anyone (most of us have this list in our head). I've had many clients start this exercise by just writing down what they have never told anyone simply to get it out of the way, and boy, did this help them get through the rest of the process.

Then, of course, I had some *ugly* things in my inventory. The ugly stuff that other people had done to me that I was not responsible for but had a negative impact on my life. I had quite a list. Physically writing out my fourth step was definitely a challenge, but I got it done in a few hours. Typically, it's not wise to bring up all this sludge in your soul without having a place to take it, because you can be triggered and feel all kinds of emotions.

I remember assigning myself this project in a hotel room at a conference where I was teaching. To do the next step when alone in the hotel, I had to tell it to myself. So, I read the list to myself out loud. Also, I knew I had to tell God. I did, and that was good. The toughest part, though, was telling another human being. This was the jumping-off-the-cliff part for me. I thought long and hard about it. There was a guy who had a sex addiction and had been in recovery. He was actually a professional counselor ministering out of his healing. I picked him for a few reasons. One, he was a believer. Two, he seemed mature. And three, he was a counselor, so I figured I would pay for the session, and he could never violate my confidentiality because it would be illegal. I booked the appointment.

I remember walking up the stairs to his small office with the heaviest couple of pages I have ever held in my life in my pocket. I sat in front of him and told him I needed to do my fifth step. Because he was in recovery himself, he knew not only what I was doing but also the sacredness of it. I went item by item, right down the three columns that were my life. He sat patiently for about forty-five of the longest minutes of my life as I went point by point. At the end of it, he said some pretty powerful things, but the most powerful thing was, "I forgive you, and I love you, and I am proud of what you did today. That took courage." I had opened the deepest parts of my heart and soul and felt accepted, not rejected. The devil had been lying to me, telling me that I would be rejected if I was honest with someone else about my secrets.

When I gave him the check for his time and wisdom, he handed it back to me and said, "This is on me. You were doing recovery, not counseling." Then, he gave me a reaffirming hug. Honestly, walking out of his office, I didn't feel much different. I was expecting something. I didn't know what, but something. I got in my little RX-7 Honda car and drove off. But when I stopped at a particular stop sign, something changed. The only way I can put it is, I had a divine encounter. It was real and hit me out of the blue. There are no words to adequately describe what happened. I'll try. It was like pure liquid light flashed through my entire body from head to toe.

Cleansing me, I felt my past mistakes fall off of my soul. The encounter was so intense that I had to pull over in a nearby field. I jumped out of the car and ran around with my hands in the air, praising the Lord with a loud voice. I was not just free. I was free indeed! Since that moment, the false guilt and shame about my story have been gone, and it's been over three decades. Why am I telling you this? Because taking these two steps allowed me to forgive myself. This is my story around the fire, so to speak.

If you endeavor to do this, choose your confessor wisely. First, think of a trusted spiritual leader who is mature and doesn't gossip. Be careful even then; spiritual leaders have been known to break confidence. If you are in recovery, someone like a sponsor would be ideal. You could do what I did and schedule a therapy appointment with a professional. If you are near Colorado Springs, see one of our amazing counselors or coaches. They know exactly what you are doing, and there's total confidentiality.

The Next Step

Earlier in the book, I referred to some forgiveness exercises that I have done with my clients to give them a tool they could use *after*—and *only* after—they do the cleansing of the temple on the person who has hurt them. I want to share that tool with you here and a few applications of this exercise. This will expedite your superpower of being able to forgive and throw those mountains into the sea of forgetfulness. In this step, you will be releasing yourself from the perpetrators who have hurt, abused, neglected, or traumatized you. We've often heard it said that forgiveness is more for us than for anyone else. My personal and professional experience concurs. Forgiveness offered after cleansing your temple of trauma is very healthy and liberating.

In this exercise, you will need two chairs and privacy. When I say privacy, I mean you need to feel safe. Make sure nobody else is home or find a secluded space. At a minimum, have the door locked so you can be undisturbed. I would have a box of tissues handy, because you are likely to encounter some strong feelings as you do this part of your Forgiveness for Everyone exercise. Turn off the phone(s) and make sure everyone is out of the house. Have the two chairs face each other.

The first of these exercises is for you to be able to address those who have hurt you. I don't want you to form an opinion about the exercise until after you go through all the perpetrators on your list. Each one can be an entirely different experience. Please do not stop here on the journey. If you're hesitant, just jump into it and those feelings will disappear. Remember, action cures fear. I have helped thousands take this step and never had one person say it was not helpful or life-changing. There are three phases to this exercise. Let's walk through each.

Phase 1: Sit in one of the chairs. We will call this "Chair A" for our discussion. From here, you will role-play the perpetrator who has hurt you. Only do one person at a time. You can use your perpetrator's name if you know it. If he or she was a stranger, you can give them a name or say, "I am the one who abused you." Acting as the perpetrator in Chair A—let's use "Fred" as an example—face the empty "Chair B" and imagine yourself sitting in it. As Fred, you can own the abuse, apologize, and ask for forgiveness. You are role-playing this, so you are using your voice to be Fred. As Fred, you might say something like, "(Your Name), I need to take responsibility and ask you for forgiveness. You were only a child, and I should have protected you. Instead, I did (name the offense) . . ." Be sure to acknowledge exactly what they did or didn't do to you that caused your pain. You might be talking for several minutes, going through all the things they did or didn't do to you. As the perpetrator, mention the cost to you. The perpetrator could say, "I know this cost you years of shame and blaming yourself or all kinds of confusion, impacting your marriage and how you didn't pursue certain goals. I take responsibility and ask you to forgive me for all these costs to you and your life."

Be specific. Don't just say, "I'm sorry." Instead, if Fred was an adult who forced you into oral sex as a child, in the role of Fred you may say something like, "I am the one who made you perform oral sex. I used you like other boys I victimized. You were just an object to me when I did this to you. I know I must have damaged your life, causing you all kinds of shame and self-hatred, which resulted in you never trusting men again. I hope you can heal, and I now ask you to forgive me."

Again, you are role-playing them as if they are having a lucid and clear moment. They are maturely taking responsibility for the pile of pain they have caused you. Do not argue that they would never do this for real. That is irrelevant. What's important is that you do this so you can take control of your life and have a chance to fully forgive them. Remember, as we talked about earlier in the book, they don't need to do anything for you to forgive them.

Phase 2: After you have role-played the perpetrator and Fred has apologized to you, physically get up and move to Chair B. In Chair B, role-play yourself as receiving this information from your perpetrator (Fred). You have just heard him apologize and ask forgiveness for the acts he did toward you and the effect they had on you.

Now, sitting in Chair B, you can respond in any way that you like. You may not be ready to release the perpetrator or forgive them at this time. That's fine. Commit to coming back to the chairs once a month until you arrive at that place of forgiveness. Staying on the journey is what's important. Whatever your thoughts or feelings are, verbalize them out loud to the perpetrator. One of the purposes of this exercise is for you to be honest. Releasing them at some point is a gift you can give to yourself. Their life moved on whether you let them off the hook or not. By forgiving and releasing them, you are not approving of what they did to you or in any way minimizing the pain they inflicted on you. You are simply releasing that behavior from having an influence in your life. However, if you were able to forgive your perpetrator, then move on to Phase 3.

Phase 3: Physically move back to Chair A and resume the role of the perpetrator. At this point, you need to respond to the forgiveness or the release that has been extended toward you as the perpetrator. Here, you are role-playing Fred, whom you just forgave. He might say something like, "(Your Name), thank you so much for forgiving me. That was huge for you to do. I truly don't deserve it, but you deserve to be free, and I am so grateful you forgave me today."

This concludes the three phases of forgiving anyone. First, do your cleansing of the temple on each person(s). Then, do this role-play exercise on them. You will be amazed at how many people on your list you can actually forgive. This is a powerful exercise for anyone to participate in. As you complete it, you can fully say goodbye to this chapter of perpetrators from your past. From this point on, the majority of people can view the abuse, neglect, or trauma as part of their history without allowing ongoing effects to continue. This is like bearing a scar from an accident but no longer suffering from the pain.

Two More to Go

If you are doing this work, you will almost certainly experience tremendous breakthroughs. It's critical that you work through each perpetrator separately and do the forgiveness exercise. After you do all your perpetrators, there are two more things to do.

Just like with the above exercise, you will need two chairs, a box of tissues, and a quiet place. Once more, have the chairs face each other, but this time, in Chair A, you are going to be your real self. In Chair B, imagine Jesus sitting there facing you. While seated in your chair, ask Jesus to forgive you for specific sins, mistakes, pain you have caused, and what you have committed toward Him—disobeying him, hurting His people, not seeking him, and causing Him pain as you walked away or did your own thing. Ask forgiveness for what you have done and how you have hurt Him. I have heard thousands of these confessions in my office with clients. They usually go something like this:

"Jesus, wow. Jesus, I really need to ask You for forgiveness. I knew You when I was young, and then I put

You on the shelf when I was in high school, wanting to be cool. I drank a little and started having sex. I truly believed I was too dirty for You, so I stopped reading the Bible, praying, and would half-heartedly go to church. Then, in college, I left You at home with my parents. I ignored You except whenever I got in trouble. I have had sex with about fifteen different people. I didn't even like some of them. Forgive me for abandoning myself like a prodigal. I had a secret porn life and secret behavior. I lied to others and pretended to be good. The first time I bought a prostitute, something died inside of me. I just couldn't reach out at all and avoided anyone who knew You. I faked it around my family and at the holidays. I've felt so alone. My lying to your daughter, my wife, is seriously sick. She is beautiful and faithful, and I crushed her when she caught me wanting to hook up with somebody on Facebook. Please, Jesus, forgive me of this and anything I have forgotten, please Jesus." At this point, there are usually tears.

After you ask for forgiveness, physically get up and switch into the Jesus chair, Chair B. His Spirit is in you, so trust the process. Here in Chair B, you role-play being Jesus as He just heard you ask for forgiveness.

Jesus died to forgive us, so He is delighted that you showed up and are owning your sin. His response usually sounds like: "Son (if it's a male like this example),

I have forgiven you, and I do forgive you. I love you. Please seek me again. I want to heal and bless you and still use you. You never left my heart or sight. I was beaten, hung on the cross, and died for you. That's how much I love you and desire to forgive you. You are forgiven of everything. Just accept my gift."

Now, after Jesus forgives you, switch back to Chair A. Then, respond to Jesus' forgiveness by telling Him "Thank you," accepting His forgiveness, and receiving it into your heart. I have worked with many believers, even pastors and ministry leaders, who say they have never before felt or actually experienced forgiveness from Jesus like that. They knew forgiveness cognitively, but doing this exercise cemented it into them that they were truly forgiven by the grace of God. If you do this work, you can experience the grace of God in such a significant manner that if you don't do this exercise, you could be robbing yourself of something life-changing.

Okay, only one more to go, and we've saved the best for last. You have been practicing your superpower of forgiveness on others, and now it's time to put it to use on the one that almost all my clients say is the hardest: yourself. To do this exercise, you will need those two chairs again, some tissues, and privacy. This time, you will start in Chair A as yourself and role-play, talking to yourself in Chair B. If "Betty" was doing the exercise, she would sit in Chair A as herself and imagine talking to herself in Chair B. Betty would be asking Betty for forgiveness for what she has done or hasn't done for herself or against herself. This is her confessing her sin to herself. It would go like this: "Betty, I need you to forgive me for . . ." Betty would work through her list of things for which she needs to be forgiven. This includes the things she didn't do to stick up for herself, set boundaries, or get an education or develop job skills; and for allowing herself to be ignored in her marriage, act like everything is okay while she's dying inside, and lie to herself that everything is okay.

When Betty in Chair A is done asking for forgiveness to the imagined Betty in Chair B, she gets up and switches chairs. Hopefully, you can forgive yourself. If not, keep coming back to this monthly, just like you did with the difficult-to-forgive perpetrators. Eventually, there will be a breakthrough, and you will be able to forgive yourself.

Back to Betty. She heard the request for forgiveness. In this case, she forgave Betty, saying: "I know you were not given much. They said you were worthless, and you treated me that way. I know you abandoned me and used my body to get love and could not open your heart. You were broken early on, and I freely forgive you for all that you have done, and I commit to start loving you from this moment on hearing what you have to say and what you are feeling."

After Betty in Chair B forgives Betty in Chair A, you switch back to Chair A as yourself (in this case, Betty) and respond with some version of thank you. "Betty, I needed to hear that you forgave me. I didn't realize what I was doing to you. Thank you for forgiving me, and I'm going to grow up from here. I love you and will show it moving forward."

When you have done all your cleansing the temple work—forgiving the perpetrators, letting God forgive you, and then forgiving yourself—you have moved some mountains. Your faith has made you whole, and you feel and believe you are forgiven. Now you have a tool set to utilize when your past tries to creep back into your future. Good job! You deserve to go get a good night's sleep. When you wake in the morning, the birds will be chirping a new melody as you breathe in some of that fresh, "I'm forgiven" air.

CHAPTER NINE

Boundaries

The fire is dying down and yawns are breaking out as some are starting to doze off from the long day of intense hiking. Nothing will wear a person out like a challenging climb in high elevation with a backpack on. Now, it's time to crawl into our tents for some much-needed shut-eye. Dawn will come soon enough, bringing with it a brand-new day of mountain adventures. Before we get zipped into our sleeping bags, however, our wise guide asks if we all have our "in case" bags in our tents. Most of us know what he means, but a few of the first-timers scratch their heads like they should have read the preparatory emails more closely.

"Remember," he gently reminds us, "we are guests of the forest and don't live here. However, there are wild creatures that do live here, so you'll need to have your 'in case' bag handy in case we get a visitor or visitors. Also, don't have open food in your tent because out here, animals will sense it. Once they smell food, they compete for it, and you'll be their main competitor." Our guide then assures us he will have all the camp's food properly stored away so as not to attract any wild animals. With our "in case" bag nearby and our food secured, we can sleep peacefully.

The "in case" bag usually includes bear spray and an air horn, which is incredibly loud and scares most creatures away. I actually keep one by my door at my home in Colorado, so whenever I head out for the woods, I won't forget to grab it. Also, bears, mountain lions, and other potentially dangerous wild animals have occasionally wandered up to the house, and I can quickly get to it. They hate that earsplitting and irritating blast. On the trail, the air horn usually works just fine, but some of us carry guns for emergencies like rattlesnakes and such. If your hike is going to be an overnighter, then it's wise to carry an "in case" bag with you.

It's also wise to have an "in case" bag when traveling on this journey of Forgiveness for Everyone. Throughout our lifetimes we will encounter a variety of people. Some will be mature, healthy, and safe. Others, regardless of their age, will be the exact opposite—immature, unhealthy, and definitely not safe. These are the wild night creatures we will all undoubtedly encounter from time to time. They are not a reflection of who we are unless we ourselves are unhealthy. As we get healthier, we tend to shed these unhealthy people. Regardless of how healthy we are, though, there are still people who are unsafe to be around or give our hearts to in any way.

Jesus was a model example for us in this. Perfect and sinless, He went around doing good, profoundly changing people's lives by setting them free from the heavy yokes of bondage they were carrying. Yet, despite who He was and all the love and compassion that flowed out of Him, there were those who acted unhealthily toward Him. They made up lies and gossiped about Him because He was a threat to them and their evil, demonic agendas. They eventually justified having Jesus murdered for something He was completely innocent of. They put guilt on Him that wasn't His to bear. What's interesting is that Jesus never allowed Himself to be the one responsible for those who came into His life, whether healthy or not.

There were occasions in Jesus' life when he maintained healthy boundaries between Himself and others. One such instance is this: *"Now while He was in Jerusalem at the Passover Festival, many people saw the signs He was performing and believed in His name. But Jesus would not entrust Himself to them, for He knew all people. He did not need any testimony about mankind, for He knew what was in each person"* (John 2:23–25).

Remember, for almost forty years, I've been counseling those struggling with sexual addiction, porn addiction, intimacy anorexia, and spouse/partner betrayal trauma. When they show up for their counseling intensives, they can be in pretty bad shape. However, as they continue in the process, which includes forgiveness, they almost always start shifting away from unhealthy dynamics toward a much healthier relationship. During this often-trying process, keeping them safe with each other is a major priority. So much so that when laying the initial foundation for the intensive, we stress and teach about the criticalness of setting healthy boundaries.

Boundaries are our "in case" bag while on this journey. As you travel, you may have already crossed paths with some people who, like creatures in the wild, are not safe. They might be immature, unskilled in relationships, self-serving, addicted, abused, or even have untreated psychological disorders. Whatever it is, they will bite you and tear your emotional flesh to bits. The only way to deal with them is to set healthy boundaries to keep you safe when these creatures come into your life.

These wild creatures can be neighbors, coworkers, church people, past relationships, or even prodigal children. We have an entire course on *Parents of Prodigals*, and in it, parents are taught how to build safe and healthy boundaries with their prodigals. Often, these people are in your immediate family, like your mom, dad, siblings, or spouse. Setting proper boundaries in these cases can be especially difficult because you live with the person and are close to them. You may have heard it said that we train people how to treat us. This is true to some degree. However, there are those who simply won't be trained regardless of how hard you try. Having the wisdom to know what healthy boundaries look like and then how to set and reinforce them is foundational to living a lifestyle of Forgiveness for Everyone.

Boundaries

When I think of boundaries, my mind immediately pictures the borders between countries. The United States is an ideal example of both healthy and unhealthy boundaries. To the north with Canada, there is mutual respect, and we both honor each other's border line. Both Canada and the US check on who is coming and going from one country to the other. On our southern border, however, it depends on who the current president is. Those crossing are aware of the border stance of the current administration and take action accordingly. Like the US border, you might have some family and friends who choose to honor your boundaries, and those who choose to push your boundaries. And, it is also up to you to enforce your boundaries on them.

Throughout the Bible, walls and boundaries were crucial. When Hanani reported to Nehemiah that the walls surrounding the city of Jerusalem were broken down, the Bible says Nehemiah wept: *"And they said to me . . . 'The wall of Jerusalem is also broken down, and its gates are burned with fire.' So it was, when I heard these words, that I sat down and wept, and mourned for many days; I was fasting and praying before the God of heaven"* (Nehemiah 1:3–4 NKJV). But why? Why did Nehemiah weep? Because as a result of the walls being broken down, the people were living in "distress and reproach." The enemy and other creatures were flooding in and corrupting the city. In response to his fasting and prayer, God told Nehemiah to rebuild the walls so the people would be safe. God is all about healthy boundaries for both nations and individuals, both physical and emotional.

Boundaries are ideally meant to protect both sides of the relationship. Sometimes, if a hostile country threatens another sovereign nation, boundaries must be protected and reinforced. We know this on an intuitive level when we feel unsafe in a situation. We are especially prone to fortify our boundaries when we sense a threat to us or those we love. Something rises up within us to protect what is ours.

As a psychologist, I have heard the term *boundaries* tossed around in many different ways. For our purposes, let's take a minute and discuss what a boundary is not. A boundary is not a guarantee of safety for anyone. A boundary is not a magic bullet to protect you from the pain of other people's behaviors against you. Boundaries are not meant to be symbolic of anything. They don't guarantee positive outcomes or that the other person's behavior will change. Boundaries are not meant to give us false hope that things will eventually be better. Human beings were created with free will and can choose to love or not to love and how they will respond. The reasons people choose certain hurtful behaviors are many and varied, but the underlying reason is we live in a broken, sinful condition. As a result, many decide to be destructive in their relationships, even intimate relationships like family or marriage. God doesn't control a person's free will, and we can't either.

Boundaries simply are you declaring plainly how you expect to be treated in a relationship. You are not being unkind or difficult; you're just being clear. All of us need to be heard and treated with respect in our relationships. Unfortunately, not everyone we are involved with comes equipped to honor our hearts. Over time, if a relationship becomes dysfunctional and devolves into an unhealthy state, boundaries become even more essential.

Generally speaking, in most relationships, you'll want to focus on one boundary at a time, especially early on. Trying to maintain more than one can be overwhelming for both parties. It will take plenty of energy to keep that single boundary until it becomes the norm in your relationship. Adolf Hitler learned this lesson of diverting his energy into more than one direction the hard way. Prior to fighting Russia, he used a method of war known as the *blitzkrieg* model. This model called for the military to identify their target and then concentrate the whole of their forces in that one location moving forward. It was when Hitler decided to divide his armies and fight on two fronts that he lost the war.

Establishing boundaries in any relationship is likely to be a bit tricky in the beginning. All relationships have operating systems that are either healthy or unhealthy. When you are attempting to alter those systems regarding how they relate to you, it can be challenging for both parties. Change doesn't come easy for some and is often not welcomed, even if it's mutually beneficial.

To start setting a new boundary, you might want to discuss what your new expectation in the relationship is so you both clearly understand. Again, you are not being unkind or difficult. If the person you are dealing with is healthy and secure, they will have no problem and will actually welcome the insight. This can help facilitate a possible mutual understanding of the potential change in the relationship, depending on the maturity level of those involved. Let's use a simple example to illustrate starting a boundary. In this case, the relationship is a marriage.

Tina and Mike have been married for nine years. They met in a bar prior to coming to Christ, and both struggled with pot and porn on and off in their marriage. Then, they got saved together at a Christian event and have been going to a good church ever since. It was a beautiful God thing. Still is. Most of the major destructive behaviors like drugs and porn stopped early on. However, they had this dysfunctional way of dealing with conflict. Mike would erupt violently, yelling and cursing at Tina to the point it would scare her and their young children. As you can imagine, she felt disrespected and degraded, so she wanted to set a boundary around Mike yelling at her. Tina took the first step with Mike and talked to him clearly and calmly about this issue of him yelling at her when he got angry during an argument.

"Mike, when the yelling happens," she explained, "I feel degraded, disrespected, and scared. It frightens our kids too." Tina first shared how she felt about the behavior and then asked Mike if he wanted her to feel this way because, after each episode, it took time for her to recover. Mike agreed that his outbursts were not a good thing. Tina asked for an agreed-upon boundary that went as follows: if either of them violated the boundary and started yelling, the person doing the yelling would have an agreed-upon alternate behavior or a consequence that they set for themselves. Mike agreed and came up with, "If I start to yell, you can say the words 'stop sign.' That will be our code for me to change my behavior or do my consequence, and I will use the same code for you." If Mike yelled and "stop sign" was used, he agreed to go to another room and read his Bible and pray for ten minutes, or he could call the man he was doing a Bible study with for help. Tina agreed this would be good and asked what the consequence would be if he didn't honor the boundary of not yelling. He promised that he would wash and detail her car that same day. Tina accepted. Mike then asked Tina what hers would be, even though it wasn't nearly as much of an issue for her.

She promised that if he said "stop sign," she would go for a fifteen-minute walk, pray, or call someone if she felt she needed to. Tina said if she didn't do this walk, her consequence would be making Mike his favorite dessert. The boundaries and rules had been set, but they failed to account for what happens if the person didn't keep their word, which definitely can happen when tempers start flaring. So, Mike said if Tina didn't take her walk or make the dessert, his response would be to not watch television with her that night, which she really enjoyed doing with him. Tina said if Mike didn't keep his word, she would not sleep in the same bed with him that night or until he detailed her car. Then, they both agreed to talk to their cell-group leaders at church and ask them to hold them accountable. These leaders had helped them in the past, and Tina and Mike both trusted them with their issues.

Steps to Healthy Boundary Setting

1. Discuss the changed behavior.
2. Set a strategy for change with a sequence of behavior (e.g., walk away instead of escalating).

3. Set your own consequence so you are doing it to yourself and not being punished by the other individual.
4. Have a plan and consequence you can enforce without the other person's involvement.

This is a safe and healthy way to go about setting and implementing specific boundaries with a spouse. Of course, it always takes two, and there's that free will thing. However, we are not always married to the people we need to have boundaries with. Sometimes, it's children, current friends, past friends, coworkers, or even people at church. Often, those we seek to have boundaries with are not keen on us having them, especially if they've been able to use us or capitalize on our lack of good boundaries in the past.

I'm thinking of the grandmother who loves her grandchildren dearly, but her daughter always wants her to watch them so she can have a life. The problem is, the grandmother's life gets smaller and smaller because of how much she is watching the grandchildren. It's not that she doesn't enjoy being with them. She does! It's just that she gets worn out, and it becomes too much.

Whenever she says "No," her daughter goes into a rage, gets entitled, cries, and blames her mom. Then, she threatens her mother with not seeing the grandchildren.

This is a highly toxic situation where the other person is immature and can get out of control quickly. The mother can state how she feels limited in her life, but her daughter doesn't care about her mom's feelings. She wants to go out with her friends, so Mom's life is not important. The daughter is using her mother like an object whom she has taken for granted and used most of her life.

In this situation, if the mom wants her daughter to treat her differently, she will have to first communicate that the "just-dropping-off-the-children" behavior is not acceptable any longer. Then, she must be willing to put up with any of the daughter's antics, including not seeing the grandchildren. She can give her daughter days and times when she is willing to watch the children with the stipulation that, if she is late picking them up, the next time will automatically be canceled so that the daughter will learn to respect her mother's time. There is no way of telling how this type of boundary setting will play out. For instance, if the daughter has an addiction, some disorder, or is simply extremely immature, she might cut the mother off completely. It may take going through some choppy waters to get to the point where the daughter values her mother as a person and is grateful for what she does for her.

As I said earlier, boundaries do not predict outcomes. If someone does not see your value, their behavior will not change and may even get worse in order to keep the old system in place, which benefits them.

Years ago, I had to set a professional boundary for myself. I really do respect the value of people, because Christ died for them. So, I'm not too keen on people yelling at each other in my office. However, I am aware that when dealing with spouses finding out about infidelity or porn or other secrets, they might go off for a bit. And rightfully so. That's not what I am talking about. What I'm talking about is when clients just scream back and forth and are not listening to each other. In a situation like that, I'll first make them aware of their behavior.

"You both are just yelling at each other, and that's not acceptable in my office." After hearing me say this, most couples regulate and start acting more mature. Others don't. If they yell at each other like that in my office, think of what they do at home. They do it so often at home that they start thinking it's acceptable adult behavior. If they continue, I will say, "If you don't stop this behavior, I will leave the office, and you both can sit here and do this, but I will not participate or validate by my presence that this is acceptable. When you are done, you can come get me. If you can talk like adults to each other, we'll continue." If they don't regulate, I leave the office, and usually, I only have to do this once for them to realize I will enforce my boundaries if need be.

Here, I am giving you an example of setting the boundary and then stating what I will do if the behavior doesn't change. I am not giving them a consequence or punishing them. I am simply making them aware of what will happen if they don't regulate themselves. Lastly, I do enforce the boundary. I am worth Christ's blood as well, because He says so. Thus, I will not accept being disrespected, even by clients.

One of the secrets to having healthy boundaries is knowing you do have worth. I've had several clients go through the *Worthy* DVD and workbook as a precursor to starting boundaries work. The reason we do this course is because if they don't believe they are worthy, they will continue to put up with being treated poorly as well as not feeling worthy enough to protect themselves. Some of my clients have had family members so dysfunctional that trying to have boundaries with them was disheartening, because the other person would not have anything to do with valuing others. They would not stop acting out of control, controlling, or crazy. So, with great sadness, my client had to distance themselves from this person or couple. It may be an in-law, a parent, or an uncle or aunt who is just toxic, plain and simple. They might treat your spouse or children with disrespect or feel they are called to give their negative opinion about anything regarding this person. Giving distance to this relationship might be necessary in some situations. I would say if you are running out of ideas, talk to your pastor or counselor or read any of the many books on boundaries and proceed as you think is wise.

Boundaries can mean change, but they can also limit some people from being a part of your life with any regularity. There is sadness about the loss of a person who is not healthy enough to be in a relationship with you. I have known couples who needed to limit contact with extended family members who were not safe for them or their children. They felt the weight of protecting their family from this person's unwillingness to honor them.

Boundaries continue to be needed in this world. Every day, we are watching our Christian values diminish along with the value of the human soul. Boundaries in relationships allow you to use your voice respectfully while expecting value and respect in return. When this doesn't happen, it becomes necessary to make your boundaries and decide as you go through life which relationships are healthy for you in each season. I wish boundaries gave us more ability to help others see and become better people, but they cannot. What they can do is allow you a way to help keep your heart soft in a world that can be hard at times.

The last way to use boundaries is on yourself. I do this all the time when I need to grow, change, or even lose weight. I start with repentance with God, self, or others. After that, I set a discipline in place to counter the behavior, like letting people complete their entire thought before I speak. This is a goal I use when I need to grow in patience. It seems to be a telltale sign of how I am doing with that fruit of the Spirit. So, I set a boundary that if I don't let someone finish their sentence before I speak, I will give myself a consequence. One consequence I use on myself is push-ups to failure. Believe me, this adds up, and you can get plenty sore the next day! I try to be more patient. I then make myself accountable to someone, and if I don't do that consequence every time, I give them twenty dollars. This discipline has been successful for me time and again, from changing behavior to losing those extra pounds. I hope this little excursion into boundaries can be helpful in your journey of Forgiveness for Everyone and keep your heart both safe and soft as you travel this mountain called life.

CHAPTER TEN

The Trail Less Traveled

"I hope you are all awake," our guide calls out while going from tent to tent to make sure we are up and at 'em, getting ready for the morning stretch of our journey. The aroma of hot coffee brewing on the fire wafts through the crisp Colorado air. Protein bars and small snacks are laid out for everyone to enjoy before hitting the trail. Brian wanders off to relieve himself and comes back all excited, as if he's seen an exotic wild animal or something. He motions for us to quickly come and see.

Everyone sluggishly scurries over toward Brian and follows him toward whatever he was so excited about. Curiously, our guide takes up the rear, which he hasn't done the entire trip. We continue tailing Brian along the boulder-sprinkled forest path. Up ahead, the trees spread open like nature's curtain and Brian stops. "This is it!" he announces. "We made it. We're at the peak. Isn't it amazing?"

With mouths stuffed with protein bars and trail mix, we can hardly believe what our eyes are viewing. Stretched before us for what must have been hundreds of miles in several directions is the most breathtaking Rocky Mountain valley. The sky is crystal clear, making the pinnacles jutting in the distance look razor-sharp. "This very spot is on my wall calendar!" someone in the group shouts.

While everyone is oohing and aahing, our guide is grinning from cheek to cheek, pleased to see people enjoying the beauty and wonder of God's creation. But he's also smiling because he knows something the rest of us don't. This is no new conversation for him. He's been here numerous times before with other excited first-time trailblazers. Gripping his coffee firmly, he walks out to the edge of the cliff, takes a deep breath, and says, "So glad you guys found this place. These incredible views are yours to take in. This is part of why we came, but welcome to what we call a *false summit*."

"A false summit?" Angela asks, still gazing in awe over the massive valley. Several others nod, indicating they are puzzled as well. The guide then shares that on these climbing ventures, it's common to hit a couple of false summits depending on the mountain. This is when it appears you are at the peak because of the angle you are at on the mountain. False summits almost always have spectacular views and are a welcome sight for weary campers, but they are not the summit. The authentic summit can still be hours away. It's not unusual for novices who don't have a knowledgeable guide to miss seeing the real summit view because they simply don't know what they don't know, and as a result, they head back down the mountain.

"Okay, guys," our guide says with a sheepish smile. "I'll admit, this is pretty awesome, but there's so much more. Let's get back, get our gear together, and though it may be hard to imagine, I'm going to show you an even better view."

Knowing that I'm going to draw a parallel here, some of you are probably thinking, *Really, Dr. Weiss? More? I read about the stop signs, drove through those. Went through what is abuse and neglect and realized that some of it applied to me. Made my list of people who hurt me. Cleansed my temple. Sweated like I couldn't imagine and came out feeling great. Then you had me forgive all of my people, including talking to God and forgiving myself. I even learned a couple things about setting boundaries with some toxic people in my life. Now you're telling me there's more. But after accomplishing so much and feeling so free, what more could there be?*

I'd give anything for you to see my face right now. I'm wearing that same grin as our guide going up the mountain, because I'm thinking, *Yep, there is more, and it's so much better than you can imagine. If you only knew what lay ahead, you'd be over the top with excitement to get it together and climb, baby, climb!*

You might have heard the saying, "Go back to go forward." Movies involving superheroes often go back to some hurt or trauma, like a spouse, child, or someone dear to them who was killed or died tragically. The hero aches from a past mistake or failure that adversely affected their loved one. They believe they caused it or possibly could have stopped it if they would have just done more. Maybe they got to the bomb seconds too late. The director often takes the viewer back several times into the hero's head as they wrestle with that familiar tormenting dream or memory. Although facing the huge weight of saving the world, they also carry the heaviness of their past issues. In some movies, the hero gets to travel back in time or go into another dimension to make things right. On occasion, traveling back allows them to accept the scar of their parents', spouse's, or child's death and not blame themselves. By going back, they can move forward.

This is where we are on our journey to the real summit. The closer we get, the steeper the climb. What's known as the "tree line" is when the trees stop growing on a mountain because there is not enough oxygen for them to live. The average trail hiker usually stops at this point. Now, don't get me wrong. Making it that far is quite an accomplishment. You would think trees dying for lack of oxygen would be a sign for humans not to proceed, but for the serious climber it's merely a marker of success noting that they are getting closer to the summit. Above the tree line, the climb is going to get notably steeper and the breathing heavier. We have to steady our resolve and pace ourselves. This is where it gets hard and not everyone follows through, but for those who do, the summit is life-altering.

The Emotional Tree Line

In the journey of forgiving everyone, we have to face the fact that, as Scripture tells us, *"all have sinned and fall short of the glory of God."* (Romans 3:23). That includes us. You don't have to live with yourself or others for very long on this planet to come to this realization. The truth is, every single one of us is flawed. We all make mistakes, and some of these mistakes are sin, and some of these sins not only hurt ourselves but others. Before starting a counseling intensive with someone, I do an intake where I ask specific questions to get a feel for where this soul or heart has been, including what they have seen, experienced, or caused in their life, so we can create a plan to heal. While it may seem ominous, it usually only takes me about fifteen minutes to get a good idea of what the soul has gone through. After doing this assessment for decades, I've learned that though the soul is complex, healing doesn't have to be.

Each of us has a unique past we've traveled through. During the earlier pages of this journey, we focused mainly on what other people have done or not done to us that creates pain in our lives. However, there is a parallel story: what you have done to others along the way. Because you have pressed forward through all the work to get to this point, you are now in a healthy place, maybe the healthiest place you've ever been, to address this steep section of the climb. You have more clarity about the past that has happened because of others, but also more clarity about the past that has happened because of you—both the good and the not so good. You have healed of so much along this journey up to this point. It's a great accomplishment that few get to experience. You should be proud of how far you have come if you have actually done the work through these previous pages.

You are probably less triggered by the things that used to easily trigger you. You probably feel lighter, sleep sounder, and just feel better overall. I know this was true for me after putting in the work, and it's been true of my clients for decades. Yet, as good as we might feel breathing in the higher mountain air, there is still more work to do if we are going to experience ultimate freedom.

Are you ready? I will warn you again, this is the trail less traveled. You are moving past the emotional tree line. This is where you must fully commit that, even if your lungs feel empty and your muscles burn and ache, you are going to get there regardless. Focus and resolve become more critical than ever, because everything within you will be screaming to give up and settle for the false summit. During the push upward, your body, soul, and will are going to be tested to the limit, revealing what you are really made of. The closer you get to the top, you'll no longer be walking but scaling through rocks like a baby crawling across the floor to get to its toy. This can't be done by emotions, but by your determination and God's empowerment. Having His word in your heart and mind, the Holy Spirit will bring passages to remembrance as you ascend.

"I can do all things through Christ who strengthens me. Philippians 4:13," you declare out loud to yourself. Perhaps you have a pocket Bible in your pack that you pull out and read from while resting on a rock. *"Do not fear, for I am with you; do not be dismayed, for I am your God. I will strengthen you and help you; I will uphold you with My righteous right hand"* (Isaiah 41:10). *"Be strong and courageous. Do not be afraid; do not be discouraged, for the LORD your God will be with you wherever you go"* (Joshua 1:9). *". . . but those who hope in the LORD will renew their strength. They will soar on wings like eagles; they will run and not grow weary, they will walk and not be faint."* (Isaiah 40:31). You can feel it. You're almost there.

Suddenly, you find yourself becoming an encourager to others. "Come on. You can do it! You're almost there. It's going to be worth it. Don't give up." You are surprised at what a cheerleader you have become, but you know you are talking to yourself as much as to them. Men in particular struggle to let others see their weariness, especially if they are traveling with their quite athletic girlfriend or wife. So, it's grit time in the journey. The great news is that thousands have made it before you, and you can make it too. There is a cloud of witnesses cheering you on, like the Bible says:

"Therefore we also, since we are surrounded by so great a cloud of witnesses, let us lay aside every weight, and the sin which so easily ensnares us, and let us run with endurance the race that is set before us . . ." (Hebrews 12:1 NKJV). Part of your race includes the endurance to follow through and finish this climb to the summit. It will take three things: commitment, grit, and staying steady as you put one foot in front of the other by faith. As your guide, I can say when I did this part of the journey, there were moments I wanted to quit, but as I stayed steady and started to feel the impact on my soul, I actually began to feel lighter inside as I continued to travel.

Your Hero Journey

To take this part of the journey, you'll need to have a map. However, this is no ordinary map. Nor is it a map that I, as your guide, can hand to you. It is absolutely unique to you. Everyone will have a different map as they go back to go forward. This is now your specific hero journey. Next, get out a pad of paper or your phone if it has a security code not known by others. In a few moments you are going to make that list of people you have sinned against in the past.

For some people like family members, spouses, parents, and children, you will most likely have a much bigger list, so let's save them for last. Before we get to those we have hurt, let's cover some possible ways we could have hurt them. These are in no particular order, and this is not a comprehensive list.

- Lying to someone
- Lying about someone
- Gossiping
- Humiliating someone
- Physical aggression
- Emotional bullying
- Taking advantage in some way
- Steeling time or something of value
- Having sinful sexual relations
- Blaming for what you now know was your issue
- Being unkind or cruel
- Cheating
- Betraying a friend
- Manipulating or using someone
- Causing physical injury
- Getting them started in drugs or alcohol
- Loving your addiction to something more than others
- Cruel words toward someone
- Withheld love, praise, touch, or even sympathy from someone

Of course, there are many others the Holy Spirit will help bring to your remembrance. For the most part, we are aware of what we have done or not done. As you make your list, ask the Holy Spirit if there is more you should put beside a certain person's name. Alright, now go to your pad of paper or phone.

To start, simply write down the name of each person you know you have harmed in some way. I'm amazed that when a soul commits to acknowledging the truth about themselves, their initial list of people often keeps growing as more come to mind. So, the first thing is to name them.

Second, with each person, write down what you have actually done or not done to them. Be specific. Either bullet points or paragraph form will work. It doesn't really matter. Just get it down. Lastly, write out as clearly as you can what needs to be said in order to take full responsibility for your behavior without mentioning in any way what they have done to you. Then, from the heart, write what you need to say to ask for forgiveness of them. For example, to a roommate in college: "I need you to forgive me for stealing money and food from you from time to time. I did not keep some of the confidences I promised I would, and I exposed your weaknesses to others to make myself look good. Leaving stuff out on the floor and not cleaning up after myself was immature, unthoughtful, and unkind. I wasn't a very good friend to you."

Once you get this done, there is one more step. That is to write out, for each person you have hurt, what they most likely felt from their experience with you. To the roommate it might go something like: "You could have felt hugely disrespected on a regular basis when I didn't take care of my side of the room. You could have felt betrayed when you knew I talked about you and violated your trust on some issues." Putting down what they could have felt can increase your empathy and give greater insight into how your behavior actually caused pain. So, make your list of people. Write out specifically what you did and take full responsibility. After that, write out how they could have felt as the result of your words or actions.

Now, let's talk about parents, spouses, siblings, children, long-term romantic relationships, and possibly long-term friendships. These are people you have known for years, maybe your whole life. For each of these, I would go through five years at a time on your paper. On the left side of the paper, spell out what you did that could have harmed them. On the right side, write what they could have felt from your behavior or attitude toward them. This might take a bit more time, but it's vital to go back like this so you can move forward into your future without any shadows from your past lurking.

I'm sure many of you are thinking, *Okay, Dr. Weiss, what are we going to be doing with all of these people we are listing and writing about?* So glad you asked. Big smile. We are going to go face-to-face with most of them. The ones you won't go face-to-face with are past romantic relationships if you are married, unless your spouse and pastor agree it can be done in a public place with no further contact. Personally, I don't recommend face-to-face meetings with past romantic relationships unless you are single. Even then, I would recommend you have the guidance of a counselor or pastor beforehand.

The second group of people you would not go face-to-face with are those whose names you don't know. This would include one-night stands, short relationships of some type, or even strangers. Lastly, you would not go face-to-face with those you have no way of contacting, or any sexual perpetrators.

With those exclusions in mind, start contacting the people on your list and informing them you would like to get together. When they ask why, tell them something to the effect of, "I was just thinking about some of the things that happened between us and, honestly, I need to own my side of things." In most cases you won't get pushback. If you do and they say no, you can do it right then over the phone. "Hey, I just need to ask you to forgive me for . . ." But if they are willing to meet, it's best to ask for forgiveness in person. Do not do any of this in writing (e.g., a letter, text, or email) or through social media. It can be misunderstood, or worse. Before you meet or talk, make sure you have your notes with you, so you are sure to cover everything.

With long-term and family relationships, set a time when you can get together. I recommend a safe place such as a quiet public area to ensure everyone behaves appropriately. If you feel safe with them one-on-one in your or their home, that's great. Then have your papers and prep them. "Listen, I have been doing some thinking, and I really need to take some responsibility for some things in the past and ask your forgiveness." They might try to minimize this, but let them know this is important for both of you to have a better relationship in the future. Ask them to give you a few minutes, and tell them that you wrote some things out. Then, go through each behavior, what you did, and how they could have felt, and ask forgiveness for each. They might get stuck on something, but it's okay if they don't forgive everything. You don't have to be forgiven to have a clear conscience about something. Give yourself plenty of time, at least an hour. They can respond anywhere from indifference to compassion, but again, we are not going for any particular outcome. We are just doing the right thing.

What about those people who we couldn't find or those romantic relationships? That's a super question. They are important to address as well, so we are going back to the chairs we used earlier. That's right, get your two chairs out. Have tissues and be alone.

In Chair A, you will be yourself with the notes you wrote concerning your actions that hurt them and how they could have felt. Do it out loud, symbolically facing the other person in Chair B as if they were sitting there. This might seem somewhat odd for you the first time, but it can be quite a powerful experience. When you are finished taking responsibility and asking for forgiveness, physically move to Chair B. You will now role-play them responding to you. In most cases they forgive, but even if they don't, this is about you taking responsibility for your actions. Again, it's not dependent on their responses. If they do forgive you, go back to Chair A (as yourself), and respond to their forgiveness with some version of thank-you.

This part of the journey is hard work, but you have already done so much work that it would be a shame to stop now. As before, when you are finished with a person, throw away or delete your writings. There is no need to keep this past. Regardless of their reactions, you have done something heroic. When I did this part, it took me about two months to get through everyone on my list. I was working and going to Bible school full time, but I am so glad I did it and, looking back, I'm so glad I did it in my early twenties. My list was significantly smaller than the lists of many of my clients who are in their fifties to seventies.

As your guide, I have seen people stop here and continue to carry their mistakes into their future. They have an assortment of reasons, but mostly it's pride, pure and simple. They don't want to humble themselves to others. Humility is perceived as a weakness, and keeping their self-image to themselves has greater value than the freedom that comes from doing this work. Here, I am reminded of two passages of Scripture: *"Humble yourselves before the Lord, and He will lift you up"* (James 4:10). And, *"My grace is sufficient for you, for my power is made perfect in weakness."* (2 Corinthians 12:9). Something remarkable happens when we humble ourselves and admit our weaknesses before God and even others. The Lord promises to empower us and lift us up. That's why Paul continued on to say, *"For when I am weak, then I am strong"* (2 Corinthians 12:10).

One of the benefits I had from doing this part of the journey of Forgiveness for Everyone is that from the moment I finished, I realized something had shifted deep inside of me. I now could face anyone from my past and look them in the eye, knowing I had taken responsibility for my side of the street. I have a clear conscience toward them and God. This clear conscience is amazing. I grew up somehow. I can't explain it completely, but I respected myself more for going back, not hypothetically or in a therapist's office, but in real time with real people. I straightened things out, and something new arose within me. I never wanted to do that again, so I am more careful toward others and strive to not create pain for them. Jabez's prayer became my life prayer: *"That You would keep me from evil, that I may not cause pain!"* (1 Chronicles 4:10 NKJV).

Your experience will be uniquely yours. However, I would take this part of the journey seriously. So seriously that if you find you are resisting the process, you have to ask yourself, *Why?* The more you resist and procrastinate, the more stuck you probably are. To get unstuck and reach your stated goal, here's a recommendation I give. It actually works for any type of goal. I use this secret weapon to harpoon any negative behavior or thoughts, as well as to reach my various goals, even like writing a book. I'm talking about *accountability*.

Here's what that can look like. I'm writing this part of the book on a plane coming back from Australia, where

I met several world Christian leaders at a conference that Daystar will air on its global network. Being married to Joni Lamb, the president of Daystar, the world's largest Christian television network, has not only been personally amazing, but it has also given me the opportunity to talk to some of the world's top Christian leaders.

While at this conference, the topic of writing a book came up with two leaders on separate occasions. So, I gave them the ins and outs of writing, but I always—and I mean *always*—add this one principle that will make the difference between a book getting done or remaining a concept that never gets birthed. That principle is *having accountability*. When it comes to new and aspiring authors, I recommend establishing specific goals and deadlines for writing, and then setting up a regular accountability call with someone they respect. It could be weekly to report their progress and set a consequence for themselves if they don't reach the stated goal. This simple act of incorporating accountability takes efficiency and productivity to another level.

When it comes to climbing this part of the mountain, if you are finding yourself thinking more about giving up than staying steady, it's time to push out all distractions and hyper-focus on making it to the summit. To make sure you get there, you might seriously consider having accountability with a peer, pastor, or mentor. They don't need to know the specifics, just that the Lord has you taking accountability for your past, and would they mind if you called them weekly to report your progress? I would not recommend a family member, spouse, or anyone of the opposite gender. They tend to be too soft on you. You want someone who can encourage you to climb the next boulder, remind you to keep going when you feel like quitting, and rejoice with you in your accomplishments. My guess would be less than 1 percent of Christians in any church actually have climbed this mountain and, to be fair, most don't even know it's a mountain to climb.

How about this thought? You could start a Forgiveness for Everyone group and become a facilitator of healing and a cheerleader for more people to actually do the hard work of forgiving everyone and experiencing the life-changing freedom that comes with it. For right now, though, just focus on putting one foot in front of the other and keep climbing. When you finally make it to the summit, you'll have so much joy that you won't be able to contain it. You know the saying, "Hurt people hurt people"? Well, the opposite is also true: "Healed people heal people." "Freed people, free people." Becoming a climbing guide for a new group allows you to be a conduit of all you have learned and let it flow into others. You will want them to enjoy the accomplishment of reaching the summit and seeing the view of their own life through new eyes.

CHAPTER ELEVEN

Your Tool Box

I think you can tell by now that I love the mountains. There's nothing better than experiencing the fresh air, the cold-water lakes and springs, and the occasional sighting of God's creatures, both big and small.

I also love, love, love sharing all of this on long hikes with friends or family. Sharing these experiences brings us closer together somehow. Countless meaningful conversations have unfolded on the mountain trails in Colorado. My hope is that you felt that way, too, as we hiked along these trails on the mountain of forgiving everyone. We have enjoyed the stop signs and embraced our superpower to forgive, as well as the command to utilize this superpower throughout our lives. We also traveled through some rough terrain, identifying those who hurt us, cleansing our temple of the trauma, and forgiving them as well (or at least we are in a known process toward being able to forgive them). We also forgave ourselves and let grace and forgiveness flow into our own hearts in a new way. We went on the side trail of owning our own sins and having no shame from our past anymore.

Wow! What a mountain we have climbed together through these many pages. I see the flashes of faces I have personally walked through this journey of forgiving everyone over the years. I hope you are wearing that same smile as these happy trailblazers who went before you. I'm like the guide who keeps after-reaching-the-summit Polaroids of past travelers pinned all over his wall.

I may never meet you personally, but I am so glad we shared this incredible journey together. If you become a guide in your church, home, or with friends, leading them to use their superpower of forgiveness, then all I can say is, "YOU ARE AWESOME!" To all for whom these pages were more than a book but a guide by a friend, I must say from the deepest parts of my heart, "I AM SO VERY PROUD OF YOU!"

You are part of a very small percentage of Christians who do the hard work of healing and forgiving others from the past. Looking ahead, from my experience over these almost forty years of doing this hike, there are a few things you might experience going forward. First, you will probably stop living in the past, or what I call living "from" the past. What I mean by that is the messages from these events "from" your past also disappear in your heart as you unhook yourself from both the trauma and the perpetrators of the trauma.

Second, you will tend to be a much more authentic person. This is because you are now more comfortable with your less-than-perfect self. You are able to say "I'm wrong" or "I'm sorry" with much more ease. If you're married, this can be a big plus to your relationship. You might also experience more patience and compassion for others who are still living from their past.

After my own trek up the mountain, my heart was not only more open, but it became softer toward others and myself, which is a much easier way to live. I began to realize my heart was real and that I needed to be wise with whom I gave it to. My heart also needed to learn how to heal more quickly from things that were harmful and toxic, and I wanted to shut them down. It's wonderful that now I can take my tools, the same ones I shared with you on this journey, and get right to work on those things.

Now, as a fellow traveler on this road to forgiving everyone and trying to keep my heart soft, I want to share with you a couple of final thoughts. The first is how important it is to know when to use your tools and superpower. Believe me, life will continue to happen with new hurts and new mistakes, bringing new wounds.

For me, when little things happen here and there, I'm usually able to forgive fairly easily, especially when I know the person was probably not intentionally trying to cause me pain. They just had a moment. However, when something continues to bother me for days or weeks, and I can't seem to shake it, I might conclude that it was done intentionally to hurt me, to lie to me, or to gossip about me to people I care about. In those cases, I usually have to dig into my tool box.

After that realization, I figure out a time when I can be home alone for a while. I'll write my anger letter, read it out loud, and cleanse my temple. Then, I do the chair work with my perpetrators. After that, I'm usually done with the issue and can move on. This process is what I was trying to describe as doing life like Marvel's Wolverine character. His enemies shoot him with bullets, and he just pushes them out. The wound heals quickly, and he moves on.

If you have done all the work in these pages, your intuition will now tell you when to do more work if something is cutting you emotionally. You might also have an experience, and this can happen serendipitously, where you have a memory or a feeling that you need to address something you've forgotten. At the time, it wasn't a big deal, but later, it suddenly popped up when you least expected it. I remember I had been in recovery for over five years when I had an aha moment that had me do a week's worth of work, cleansing my temple and forgiving more people. If these come up, it is a sign of health and that you are desiring to heal something. If that happens, just go with it and heal. Hit it straight on.

I was sitting with Betty, a thirty-seven-year-old Christian mother. She was head of the PTA, a successful real estate agent, and generally full of life. She had come to see me because since her daughter had turned fifteen, Betty was having all kinds of weird symptoms, including thoughts and dreams about a date rape back when she was that age. These memories had been so removed from her life that she didn't remember even thinking about the assault after high school. It didn't cross her mind again until her fifteen-year-old daughter wanted to go to a party. At that point, the memories flooded Betty's soul like a tidal wave. Betty is not alone. It is not uncommon to have something trigger a traumatic memory years—and even decades—later.

Dan was doing great in his sex-addiction recovery for over two years. He passed his polygraphs to be clean and rebuilt his marriage. Everything was going well with him until he watched the movie *The Prince of Tides*, which depicts a young boy being sexually abused. Dan had forgotten about an incident of being violated in a bathroom by a much older man. This memory had been pushed down and was encapsulated until the movie triggered it. When these things happen, your soul is saying it's time to go ahead and use your tools and process this, or even start going to counseling.

The Journey to the Summit of Peace and Freedom

Doing all the work that it took to reach the summit of Forgiveness for Everyone was no doubt a rigorous journey. Yet, mountain climbers love challenges and look forward to the adventure, so we enjoyed the trek together. Still, for this particular climb, it took everything that was in us and more.

The truth is, completing this hike to the top was bigger than our ability to pull it off alone. It took the grace and power of God, the superpower of the Holy Spirit, and the help of others. Attempting a climb alone is not wise and can lead to getting off course, which can be deadly. God didn't create us to be loners wandering in the rocky wilderness. God must empower us, and He often does that through His people. At times we need the help of others to encourage us and even pull us along, like accountability partners. One of the things I know for sure from my years of counseling is that the Lord is the great provider, and He will faithfully place people in our lives at the right time.

Without the Lord, we are nothing. Jesus said, *"I am the vine, you are the branches. He who abides in Me, and I in him, bears much fruit; for without Me you can do nothing"* (John 15:5 NKJV). We can do nothing without His life flowing through us, but with Him we bear much fruit. *"But the fruit of the Spirit is love, joy, peace, forbearance, kindness, goodness, faithfulness, gentleness and self-control. Against such things there is no law"* (Galatians 5:22–23). One commentator said, "Kindness. This fruit of the Spirit is a natural result of love. When God's Spirit begins to develop love in the Christian's heart, treating others with kindness, compassion, and forgiveness follows."[9] Walking in true Forgiveness for Everyone, including ourselves, is the ultimate peace and freedom we can ever experience, and it's found at the summit!

The Biblical Foundation of Forgiveness for Everyone

The following passage from the Gospels sets out the truths we have been pursuing on our trek up the mountain, so it seems only fitting to end our time together by quoting the words of our Savior in their beautiful entirety.

> *But to you who are listening I say: Love your enemies, do good to those who hate you, bless those who curse you, and pray for those who mistreat you. If someone slaps you on one cheek, turn to them the other also. If someone takes your coat, do not withhold your shirt from them. Give to everyone who asks you, and if anyone takes what belongs to you, do not demand it back. Do to others as you would have them do to you.*
>
> *"If you love those who love you, what credit is that to you? Even sinners love those who love them. And if you do good to those who are good to you, what credit is that to you? Even sinners do that. And if you lend to those from whom you expect repayment, what credit is that to you? Even sinners lend to sinners, expecting to be repaid in full. But love your enemies, do good to them, and lend to them without expecting to get anything back. Then your reward will be great, and you will be children of the Most High, because He is kind to the ungrateful and wicked. Be merciful, just as your Father is merciful.* (Luke 6:27–36)

CHRISTIAN RESOURCES

Worthy: Exercises and Step Book

The *Worthy* workbook and DVD is designed for a 12-week study. Here is a path that anyone can take to get and stay worthy. Follow this path, and you, too, will make the journey from worthless to worthy, just as others have.
DVD $29.95
BOOK $29.95

Emotional Fitness

Everyone has an unlimited number of emotions, but few have been trained to identify, choose, communicate, and master them. More than a guide for gaining emotional fitness and mastery, in these pages you will find a pathway to a much more fulfilling life.
BOOK $16.95

Letters to My Daughter

A gift for your daughter as she enters college, *Letters to my Daughter* includes Dr. Doug Weiss's daily letters to his daughter during her first year of college. The letters are about life, God, boys, relationships, and being successful in college and life in general.
BOOK $14.95

Indestructible

The *Indestructible* series gives you a foundational understanding of your innate design as God's child. The trials in our lives can trigger feelings of worthlessness and defeat. God's Word reveals that your soul is not capable of being destroyed. Once you recognize and embrace this, you can change how you think and feel about your past, present, and future.
DVD $29.95

Finding Grace After Abortion

In this Christian teaching series, Dr. Doug Weiss provides a safe space to explore, process, and release your pain. *Finding Grace After Abortion* is a compassionate, therapeutic teaching series specifically tailored for

Christian women who are experiencing regret, shame, and struggles that arise after having an abortion.
COURSE $49.99

Get a Grip

The *Get a Grip* book gives you the power to take control of things that are controlling you. It helps readers discover the source of their behaviors, learn how to let go of secrets, and become an accountable, responsible adult who is finally empowered to live a life of freedom.
BOOK $19.99

For more information, visit
www.drdougweiss.com/store or call 719.278.3708

MARRIAGE RESOURCES

Lover Spouse

Lover Spouse helps you understand marriage from a Christ-centered perspective. Christian marriages were designed to be different, passionate, fulfilling, and long lasting.
BOOK $13.95

Upgrade Your Sex Life

Upgrade Your Sex Life actually teaches your own unique sexual expression that you and your partner are pre-wired to enjoy. Once you learn what your type is, you can communicate and have sex on a more satisfying level.
BOOK $16.95

Servant Marriage

Servant Marriage is a revelation on God's masterpiece of marriage. In these pages, you will walk with God as He creates the man, the woman, and His masterpiece called marriage.
BOOK $16.95

Marriage Mondays

This is an eight-week marriage training course that actually gives you the skills to have a healthy, more vibrant marriage. Each week Dr. Weiss tackles major aspects of marriage from a biblical perspective. Apply these techniques and it will transform your marriage. This course helps couples to grow their marriages either in a small-group setting or on their very own private marriage retreat.
DVD $59.95

Intimacy: A 100-Day Guide to Lasting Relationships

The *Intimacy: A 100-Day Guide to Lasting Relationships* book gives you a game plan to improve your relationships. Intimacy doesn't need to be elusive! It's time to

MARRIAGE RESOURCES

recognize intimacy for what it is: a loving and lifelong process that you can learn and develop.
BOOK $22.95

Miracle of Marriage

God made your marriage to be an amazing and unique miracle. Dr. Weiss walks you through the creation and maintenance of your marriage. Yoo will be exposed to practical insights that can help make your marriage into God's original design.
BOOK $12.95

PRODIGAL PARENT PROCESS RESOURCES

Prodigal Parent Process: Full Set

The *Parent Prodigal Process* set unveils several causes for a child being a prodigal and helps you therapeutically work through deep-rooted struggles related to being the parent of a prodigal. This series will prompt serious internal dialogue within yourself as it relates to your prodigal child.
COURSE $94.85

Prodigal Parent Process Book

Dr. Weiss, drawing upon his thirty-plus years of experience working with prodigals and parents of prodigals, delivers biblical and practical tools to aid you in your

journey to hope and healing. You can't change the fact that you have a prodigal, but you can set your mind on how you will go through this journey with your prodigal.
BOOK $19.95

Prodigal Parent Process Workbook

In conjunction with the *Prodigal Parent Process* videos, this workbook helps you therapeutically work through deep-rooted struggles related to being a parent of a prodigal. This series and workbook will prompt serious internal dialogue with yourself as it relates to your prodigal child.
WORKBOOK $14.95

Prodigal Parent Process DVD

Dr. Weiss, drawing upon his thirty-plus years of experience working with prodigals and parents of prodigals, delivers biblical and practical tools to aid you in your journey to hope and healing. You can't change the fact that you have a prodigal, but you can set your mind on how you will go through this journey with your prodigal.
DVD $59.95

PARTNER BETRAYAL TRAUMA

Partner betrayal trauma is relational trauma which is created by broken trust, unfaithfulness, and a loss of confidence in your partnership, relationship, or marriage. This trauma can be caused by things like spousal neglect, cheating, infidelity, dishonesty, deception, romantic relationship betrayal, rejection, or other circumstances which cause you to lose faith in your partner or significant other.

The book, DVD set, workbook, and step guide were designed to help walk you thoughtfully through your own personal healing from the effects of being betrayed by your spouse or significant other. The pain and trauma of being betrayed, especially sexual betrayal, by a spouse or significant other, is multidimensional and multifaceted. Your pain and trauma are real, and these resources will help you in your journey of recovery from Partner Betrayal Trauma.

BOOK $22.95
DVD $65.95
WORKBOOK $39.95
STEP BOOK $14.95

SERIES FOR MEN

Clean

Every Christian man is born into a sexual war. The enemy attacks the young, hoping to scar them permanently and leave them ruined. Your past is not enough to keep you from the enduringly clean life you want and deserve. This series can be used individually or in a small-group setting.
Book $16.99
DVD $29.95
Journal $14.99

Lust-Free Living

Every man can fight for and obtain a lust-free lifestyle. Once you know how to stop lust, you will realize how weak lust really can be. God gave you the power to protect those you love from the ravages of lust for the rest of your life! It's time to take it back!
BOOK $13.95
DVD $23.95

Men Make Men

Dr. Weiss takes listeners by the hand and walks them step-by-step through the creative process God uses to make every man into a man of God. This practical teaching on DVD, combined with the *Men Make Guidebook*, can revitalize the men in any home or local church.
DVD $29.95
GUIDEBOOK $11.95

Recovery Resources

Recovery for Everyone helps addicts fight and recover from any addiction they are facing. Learn truths and gain a biblical understanding to break the strongholds in your life.

SERIES FOR MEN

You will also find an explanation as to how an addiction may have become a part of your life and details as to how you can walk the path to recovery. You will find a road map to help you begin and navigate an incredible journey toward freedom. Then you can become part of the solution and even help others get free as well.

BOOK $22.95
DVD $99.00
WORKBOOK $39.95
STEP BOOK $14.95

In a world where dating often starts with a click or a swipe, finding a genuine Christian man can feel like searching for a needle in a haystack. While they may seem scarce, they do exist, and they do hope, just like you, to find a life partner who shares their faith and values.

Whether you're a teenager just beginning your dating journey, a widow looking to move forward, or anywhere in between, this resource is designed for you.

Dr. Doug Weiss, a licensed psychologist with decades of experience in relationship counseling, offers invaluable insights that every woman should have before saying "I do." With *Finding Mr. Right*, you will be empowered to find the man of your dreams.

COURSE $79.90
WORKBOOK $19.95
DVD $59.95

Counseling Sessions

Many of our clients start seeing us because they are at a crossroads, struggling with feelings of hopelessness and battling feelings of anger, trauma, or relationship issues. We recognize the courage it takes for you to seek help, and because of this, we have a distinct approach to therapy. Our Christian clinicians don't just address symptoms; we dive deep to uncover and process the root causes of your unique situation, offering you actionable tools, exercises, and solutions tailored to your needs. Our team understands your challenges, and we are here to provide practical strategies to process and understand the root of your struggles and help you move forward.

Intensive Sessions

Are you feeling overwhelmed by trauma, sexual addiction, betrayal, or struggles in your relationship? If you're ready for a deeper level of healing, our Intensive Counseling Program offers accelerated support tailored to meet your specific needs. Whether you're navigating personal challenges or issues in your marriage, our team of experienced therapists is here to help you make meaningful progress in a short amount of time. Don't wait to get the help you need. Reach out today for more information about our Intensive program by calling (719) 278-3708. We're here to walk with you on your healing journey.

For more information,
visit www.drdougweiss.com or call (719) 278-3708

CERESET™

Heart to Heart Counseling Center has recently acquired Cereset, the most technologically advanced neuromodulation software available. It has received thirteen peer-reviewed publications and nine Institutional Review Boards (IRB) clinically approved trials, including with the US military.

By rebalancing and recalibrating the brain, neuromodulation has helped anxiety, PTSD, trauma, sleeplessness, addiction, low-mood energy, TBI, stress management, and neuroplasticity in many of our clients. Most spouses at Heart to Heart Counseling Center have many of the PTSD symptoms from betrayal. More than 80 percent of those with addiction have unresolved traumas as part of their story.

The brain is your central command center. When your brain is out of balance, or stuck, you don't feel right, and it's impossible to function at your highest level. Cereset is a proven technology that's noninvasive and highly effective. Cereset can help your brain free itself, enabling you to achieve higher levels of well-being and balance throughout your life.

Here's what clients had to say about Cereset Garden of the Gods after their sessions:

"I'm waking up earlier and feeling more rested and alert. Anxiety is lessened. PTSD symptoms alleviated. Lessened food cravings and quantity of food reduced. Arthritis symptoms improved. I feel more relaxed, less angry and reactive."

"Cereset helped save our marriage. My husband and I both did Cereset, and with it helping both of us be more calm and sleep better, we respond to each other in a more loving and respectful way. I notice a big change in him and he says the same about me. After the sessions, I noticed a marked improvement in my sleep and my ability to stay calm during moments that would trigger an argument with my spouse prior to Cereset. Before Cereset we felt chaotic, but now we both feel more at peace. Our household is a calm place to be, and we are so grateful!"

The cost for five sessions (one per day) is $1,500.
For more information, call us at 719.278.370.

ABOUT THE AUTHOR

DR. DOUGLAS WEISS is a licensed psychologist and the executive director of Heart to Heart Counseling Center in Colorado Springs, Colorado. As director, Dr. Weiss maintains a number of counselors, support groups, and three- and five-day intensive workshops. Dr. Weiss is also the president of the American Association for Sex Addiction Therapy (AASAT). Dr. Weiss is a frequent guest in the national television, radio, and print media sectors and a prolific writer on marriage, addiction, and self-help topics pertaining to intimacy in marriage, singlehood, men's and women's issues, and recovery from addiction. He is also an international conference speaker on healthy marriages and men's recovery.

NOTES

1. Doug Weiss, *Partner Betrayal Trauma: A Recovery Guide for Partners in Relationships with Sex Addicts* (Colorado Springs, CO: Discovery Press, 2019).
2. Douglas Weiss, *Finding Grace After Abortion Workbook* (Colorado Springs, CO: Discovery Press, 2024).
3. Doug Weiss, *Sex, Men, and God: A Godly Man's Roadmap to Sexual Success* (Lake Mary, FL: Siloam Press, 2011).
4. Douglas Weiss, *Worthy* (Colorado Springs, CO: Discovery Press, 2016).
5. Douglas Weiss, *Recovery for Everyone* (Colorado Springs, CO: Discovery Press, 2015).
6. Niche, "2024 Healthiest Cities in America," Niche, https://www.niche.com/places-to-live/search/healthiest-cities/s/colorado/.
7. Douglas Weiss, *Intimacy: A 100-Day Guide to Lasting Relationships* (Colorado Springs, CO: Discovery Press, 2023).
8. Matthew Henry, *Matthew Henry's Commentary on the Whole Bible: Complete and Unabridged in One Volume* (Peabody, MA: Hendrickson Publishers, 1991).
9. Compassion International, "Fruit of the Spirit," *Compassion International*, https://www.compassion.com/christian-faith/fruit-of-the-spirit.htm?utm.